JEPPE VILSTRUP H

CONNECTIVITY IS BROKEN!

NOW WHAT?

HOW TO CONNECT YOUR PEOPLE FOR BETTER PERFORMANCE AND WELLBEING

INNOVISOR CONSULTING APS
Denmark

Innovisor Consulting Aps

Jernbaneplads 1, 1st floor

2800, Kongens Lyngby, Denmark

First published in Denmark, January 2024

Library of Congress Cataloguing-in-Publication data has been applied for

ISBN: 978-87-974903-4-1

For years I have lived the power informal networks and communities. I have experienced first-hand how they could shape performance and wellbeing.

As the pandemic hit in 2020, it became evident that those informal networks and communities, were even more critical than I first thought.

Also, for me personally.

None of us are anything without our close friends and family. Regretfully, those important connections are often forgotten in our pursuit of the next big thing, the next big adventure, or the next big project at work. We make up excuses that take away time from spending time with the most important people in our lives.

This book builds on so many Innovisor projects that I have been engaged in for the past 15 years. The learnings, insights, and data shared in the book would not have been possible without the many great leaders who trusted Innovisor as their wingwoman/wingman, when they aimed to improve connectivity. I would like to thank all of you. It has been an honor.

Big thanks go to Nick Creswell, Global Head of Culture & Talent at Ørsted, John Crawford, Vice President, and Head of Human Resources at Straumann Asia, Fabrice Gallou, Distinguished Scientist at Novartis Pharma, and Hemerson Paes, Senior Global Network Catalyst at Roche.

Through in-depth interviews they provided me with valuable practical context, information, ideas, and insights, which is used throughout the book.

The Innovisor team is not to be forgotten. They have helped with wording, editing, formatting, questions, visualizations, data analysis and ideas. A great team always perform better… and we have the greatest team in Innovisor. I am humbled to have the colleagues I have in Innovisor. Thank you.

Lastly, I would like to thank my close friends and family. You know who you are. I cherish every second I spend with you. It fills me with such joy and pride that I am able to be in your lives. I look forward to sharing more moments and memories with you.

Finally, I hope you, dear reader, will enjoy the book. I hope this book will help you pursue connectivity in and outside your work life.

Don't postpone!

CONTENTS

CHAPTER ONE WHY DO WE NEED CONNECTIVITY?

"The shortest distance between two people is a smile."

– Victor Borge

Chapter 1: Why Do We Need Connectivity?

"How are you?" "Amazing to see you!"

I was always late for training in the local running club. I had exactly 30 minutes to rush ten minutes home on my bicycle, change out of my suit, shirt, and tie, put on my running gear, and then run five minutes to get to training.

I was so late that my only warmup was the bicycle ride and the short run to get there.

Stressful? – You bet!

My Big Brother Away From Home

Despite the stress of getting there, I never missed one single training session because once I finally got there, I was greeted with smiles and hellos from what I had come to consider my tribe in Copenhagen. This was the place where I could re-energize and just be myself.

Specifically, my friendship with Kjeld grew fast. He was always the first to welcome me with a big, energizing smile when I arrived. I guess you can say, he also teased me like a big brother would. "Are you late again?" Yes, I am late again. As every time.

When I arrived in Copenhagen at the age of 19, I didn't know anybody!

It felt very lonely, and it was clear I had to do something, so I joined the local running club to cope with the lack of social connections. Kjeld was there from day one. We somehow connected, while running for 45 mins from Østerbro to the Danish Aquarium north of Copenhagen and back and started to talk during the stretching.

Two Opposites Connected by a Shared Passion

On paper, he could not have been more different than me. A true Copenhagener. A fast speaker. Had never worn a tie. In general, a bit rebellious. Five to six years older than me.

I was the opposite. The silent type. Had moved to Copenhagen from a small rural town four hours away for a graduate position at one of the biggest companies in the world. The suit and tie were my new uniform. I did things by the book and had top grades.

However, we shared the same passion for being active – preferably running – and we had the same quirky humor. It created an immediate connection.

Kjeld quickly got me integrated into the running club. The social beers on a Thursday, the takeaway pizzas in the park, the fun runs on the weekend, the cake baking (and eating!) competitions, and soon also the social weekend trips.

In the business world, you would have called him my mentor.

To me he was much more than that.

He was a better long-distance runner than me but could never beat me in a 5k.

Who cared? What mattered was that we could run together. We both became faster by having a training partner that we enjoyed being around.

Running side-by-side multiple times per week. Often without sharing any words.

Our girlfriends also connected over the years, and we became personal friends.

Connected by Shared Stories and Fun

In the coming six years, I lived and worked in Germany, Netherlands, Estonia, and USA… but I always prioritized to see my tribe in the running club when I was back in Denmark. It had become part of my identity.

Nothing could keep me from the social weekends, where I often played chess with Kjeld. He was a far better player than me. I was above average, but just not at his level.

As an overconfident youngster, I had challenged him and everybody else to a game of chess the first time I took part. Kjeld took the challenge without mentioning to me that he was a competitive chess player and beat the hell out of me.

I laughed and he laughed. It was so obvious how stupid I had been. So, we kept playing! As true friends!

We All Need Friends Like Kjeld!

In 1938 a group of scientists decided to research what the ingredients of a happy and healthy life are. Their longitudinal study, which is known as the 'Harvard Study of Adult Development' still runs today, more than 80 years later.

Its conclusion is that close relationships – like my one with Kjeld – matter more than money or fame to keep people happy throughout their lives.

Close relationships protect people from life's discontents, help delay mental and physical decline, and are better predictors of happy lives than social class, IQ, or genes.

Close Relationships Make Us Healthier

Health organizations have now picked up on the incredible value of social connections and actively communicate that those social connections help:

- Mental Health: Being part of a group or community helps you survive in tough times.
- Physical Health: Communities with activities and places to gather reduce isolation and loneliness, obesity, hypertension, and diabetes.
- Longevity: You are 50% less likely to die in the next year, if you belong to a group.
- Recovery of communities after emergencies: You can build back buildings after disasters, but what matters most is to build back connection, social capital, and the vibrancy of the places again. The goal is not to build back better, but instead to rebuild the community.

With good reason, social scientists emphasize the profound effects of loneliness, revealing that its impact on mortality is equivalent to smoking 15 cigarettes per day, according to research.

So, what can you do to prioritize connectivity?

Here is what Health Organizations recommend:

1. Get to know people in your neighborhood. Offer your help when you can!
2. Develop at least three close relationships. Relationships where you can ask for help, like going to a doctor.
3. Talk face-to-face rather than through social media messaging.
4. Get involved in a cause that is important to you.
5. Join a club, team, or group, where you can live, learn, and play.

It sounds so easy. It is not! Far from it.

When Connectivity Is Too Fragile

One day Kjeld did not show up to the training. Nobody knew why, so I called him. I had so many things to share with him.

"I have been diagnosed with terminal cancer. I only have a few months!"

I was shocked and devastated.

I insisted on visiting him immediately. Just to be there. Two weeks later his girlfriend left him. She could not cope with his circumstances. I stayed around.

Kjeld was not in his usual good mood. Not cracking any jokes. With good reason. But our friendship was more important. At least I could hold his hands some of the time, run errands, and offer him comfort and a listening ear, while he talked about how he wanted his funeral to be and who was supposed to inherit what and why.

After nine months Kjeld said goodbye to the world.

I was wrecked. I still am.

Shortly after, I quit the running club. The connection was broken. I did not have three close relationships to the club (as recommended by the Health Organizations I mentioned before). I only had one.

Life Got in the Way of My Connectivity

It took more than 20 years before I again felt I had the same level of connectivity.

Not that I didn't need it, but life got in my way.

- It was difficult building true connectivity when I was holding managerial roles.
- It was difficult to find the time to prioritize connectivity, while my three kids were growing up.
- It was hard for me to build close relationships, after a serious betrayal by a person I trusted, which had huge financial consequences.

I am still not achieving all five of the recommendations from the health organizations.

More like three out of five. But I am getting there…and I will strongly recommend you do the same. If you have it already, then make sure to nurture it.

Connectivity Is Broken in Our Society

This book delves into the dynamics of broken connectivity within organizations, exploring its impact on challenges such as Mergers & Acquisitions (M&A) integration, Diversity, Equity, & Inclusion (DEI), hybrid and remote work, decision-making, teamwork, and other critical aspects.

The book will provide previously unpublished Innovisor evidence on how connectivity is broken inside organizations. It not only identifies these challenges but also charts a path towards enhanced connectivity, ultimately fostering improved performance, heightened engagement, and overall wellbeing.

It is up to ALL OF US to fix this!

Just a single daily conversation with a friend has a remarkable effect—it boosts happiness and reduces stress. The impact on wellbeing is immediate and significant!

Hence, we can only do it together! I hope you will join me.

Lessons Learned & Takeaways:

Chapter 1 explores the journey of finding connectivity through a local running club in Copenhagen. The chapter highlights the impact of social connections on mental and physical health, longevity, and recovery from emergencies, setting the stage for the book's exploration of broken connectivity in society and organizations.

1. **Close Relationships Vital for Happiness and Health:** Close relationships are crucial for happiness and health, offering support, resilience, and longevity, as emphasized by the 'Harvard Study of Adult Development.'

2. **Social Connections Mitigate Loneliness and Stress:** Connections play a vital role in reducing loneliness, stress, and promoting mental and physical health.

3. **Book Explores Broken Connectivity, Suggests Solutions:** The chapter sets the stage for the book's exploration of broken connectivity within organizations, containing insights and solutions to address challenges in areas such as teams, cross-connectivity, mergers & acquisitions, and diversity, equity, & inclusion.

Test Your Readiness – Do You Need Connectivity?

What is the likelihood of you needing to embrace more and better connectivity? Is there a high probability that the level and quality of your connectivity harms your wellbeing? Are you in the win, worry, or woe zone?

How satisfied are you with the depth and number of your close relationships or friendships?	**Very** ☐	**Somewhat** ☐	**No** ☐
How often do you engage in face-to-face conversations or activities with friends or family members, as opposed to relying solely on digital communication?	**Frequently** ☐	**Occasionally** ☐	**Rarely** ☐
How often have you participated in group activities or events that align with your interests and passions?	**Regularly** ☐	**Occasionally** ☐	**Rarely** ☐
How likely are you to seek advice or assistance from others?	**Very likely** ☐	**Somewhat likely** ☐	**Not Likely** ☐
How would you rate the impact of your social connections on your happiness and stress levels?	**Positive** ☐	**Neutral** ☐	**Negative** ☐
	Win zone	**Worry zone**	**Woe zone**

References & Further Reading to Chapter 1

- Christakis, N.A., & Fowler, J.H. (2011) *Connected: The Surprising Power of Our Social Networks and How They Shape Our Lives – How Your Friends' Friends' Friends Affect Everything You Feel, Think, and Do*, Little Brown Spark, ISBN: 978-0316036139
- Mikhail, A. (2023) Loneliness Is a Health Crisis Comparable to Smoking Up To 15 Cigarettes a Day. Here's How To Combat It, in: Fortune, available on: https://fortune.com/well/2023/06/15/loneliness-comparable-to-smoking-up-to-15-cigarettes-a-day/
- Mineo, L. (2017) Good Genes Are Nice, But Joy Is Better, in: The Harvard Gazette, available on: https://news.harvard.edu/gazette/story/2017/04/over-nearly-80-years-harvard-study-has-been-showing-how-to-live-a-healthy-and-happy-life/
- University of Kansas (2023) Just One Quality Conversation With a Friend Boosts Daily Well-Being, in ScienceDaily, available on: https://www.sciencedaily.com/releases/2023/02/230202135217.htm

CHAPTER TWO DANGERS OF BROKEN CONNECTIVITY IN ORGANIZATIONS

"Organizations are communities of human beings, not collections of human resources."

– Henry Mintzberg

Chapter 2: Dangers of Broken Connectivity in Organizations

Three Times is the Sweet Spot for Connectivity

Three times in my work life, I have worked in organizational set-ups, where high connectivity led to peak performance and then suddenly both connectivity and performance dropped.

- The first time as general manager in a small Estonian shipping agency, which grew from seven to 22 people within a year. Partly aided by the economic environment in a small country having escaped the constraints of communist Russia. The company got recognized as one of the fastest growing companies in the country, and then after splitting in to functional and informal silos fell apart as an ego-centric performance culture suddenly emerged.
- The second time in a 150-person Danish professional services organization working from the same location. Connected by the shared identity created from having been sold to new Norwegian owners. As the new owners tightened the financial grip on the organization, stress grew, divides between people enlarged, and togetherness broke down. Especially so after a move to a new office, which created larger separation.

- The third time, when a small tightly knitted group within a professional services organization grew from 15 to 35 people within two years. The leadership was tightly knit and very homogenous. However, it couldn't avoid the silos popping up as it grew, in the form of two, then three, then four teams. And then informally fell apart despite a heavy focus on staying connected.

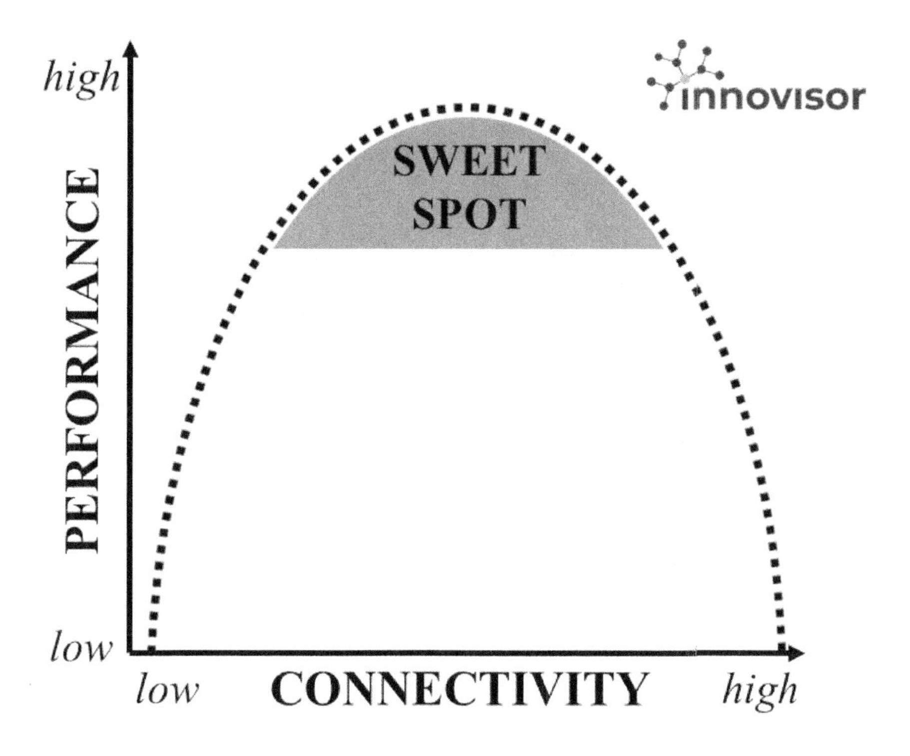

Figure 1: In the sweet spot connectivity meets wellbeing AND innovation and performance happens.

In all three cases, the complexity of the team grew either through more people, new stakeholders, or outside demands. I am sure we could have retained the peak performance if we had been better at working with people; if we had built the right conditions for them to flourish.

There are, however, certain elements you cannot escape when you work with people in organizations. The best system, the best structure, and the best process only has a marginal impact on improvement of connectivity.

The solution is still the people and how they connect to each other.

As Packard's Law states: "No company can grow revenues consistently faster than its ability to get enough of the right people to implement that growth and still become a great company."

People's Brains Are Still Wired Like Apes

You cannot avoid British anthropologist Robin Dunbar if you want to understand how people connect (and do not connect) to one another. Together with his group of researchers, he has shown that our brains are still wired as our ancestors the apes.

We might have gained new tools in the form of phones, e-mails, and social media. But the number of people we can connect to and cope with within our brains is still the same.

Dunbar has especially been noticed for the number 150, which the number of people our brain can have meaningful connections to. This rule of 150 remains true for early hunter-gatherer societies as well as a surprising array of modern groupings: offices, communes, factories, residential campsites, military organizations, and 11th Century English villages.

Exceed 150, and a group is unlikely to last long or cohere well.

The Dunbar Circles

But 150 alone doesn't tell the whole story.

Other numbers are also important. According to Dunbar, you can look at your connections as circles.

- The tightest circle has just five people – your loved ones.
- The next circle has about 15 people – good friends.
- Then 50 – your more distant friends.
- 150 - meaningful contacts.
- 500 – acquaintances.

- 1500 - people you recognize.

People migrate in and out of these layers. The idea is that your brain has a maximum capacity in each of the circles, so space must be carved out for any new entrants.

Organizations Organize According to Dunbar

Some forward-thinking organizations have organized themselves according to the Dunbar circles. The Swedish Tax Authority, for instance, has restructured their offices to stay within the 150-person threshold.

Similarly, W.L.Gore & Associates – a company repeatedly recognized as a "best company to work for" – limits its production plants to 150 people. As they say: "We found again and again that things get clumsy at a hundred and fifty."

Growth – One Enemy of Connectivity?

There is no doubt that as organizations scale, they get challenged by increasing fragmentation. Just like I experienced twice right after hitting what I considered peak performance. We added too many people to the same group. Siloes popped up and performance went down.

But why is that?

The Danger Zones Where Your Teams and Organization Fail

As teams and organizations scale most fail. In fact, less than 5% of organizations succeed in scaling above the normal start-up size.

To succeed in scaling you must grow well through specific danger zones.

Complexity Grows Exponentially with Size

Consider the simplicity of a small team with two people. The business plan could be written on the back of a napkin and what you are trying to achieve is visible in every decision. In such a team, confusion can still occur. Even though it is just a two-way channel of communication. Anyone with experience from a relationship knows that communication between two people is sometimes complex when you try to align expectations.

Add a third person to the equation and the degree of relationship complexity triples from two to six.

Add a fourth person, and it quadruples to 24.

If a team expands from three to four people, the team itself grows by **33%**.

Yet, the relationship complexity increases by **400%!**

And it keeps growing exponentially, as the organization grows.

Danger Zones Are Defined by Number of People – Not Revenue!

The danger zones for scale-ups are therefore defined by the number of its people, not by its revenue. Any experienced leader with an employee count knows how it feels to be in these danger zones.

It is where you are likely to feel a bit stuck and missing out on your agile spirit. Everything seems to take longer to complete. Decisions need to be taken in meetings. Problems you thought you had solved earlier start creeping up again. And you feel the "we-are-big-but-not-big-enough" syndrome sneaks in.

So, Where Are the Danger Zones?

In Innovisor, we have identified three zones that are more difficult to grow through and where organizations are at risk. These danger zones kick in on three stages of growth (and yes, they are not surprisingly very similar to the circles identified by Dunbar.)

15-20 people

This is the size of an organization where people know each other's hobbies but start to split into groups.

40 to 50 people

This is the size of an organization where people know each other's names, but the coherence is lost, siloed groups are clearly visible, alignment evaporates, and people do not have complete visibility into the expertise available in the organization.

125 to 175 people

This is the size of an organization where people know each other's faces and will say hi, if they meet a colleague in the supermarket. Fragmentation has set in. Groups cluster together informally and develop their own identities. Expertise's become invisible. Reinventing the wheel becomes the norm.

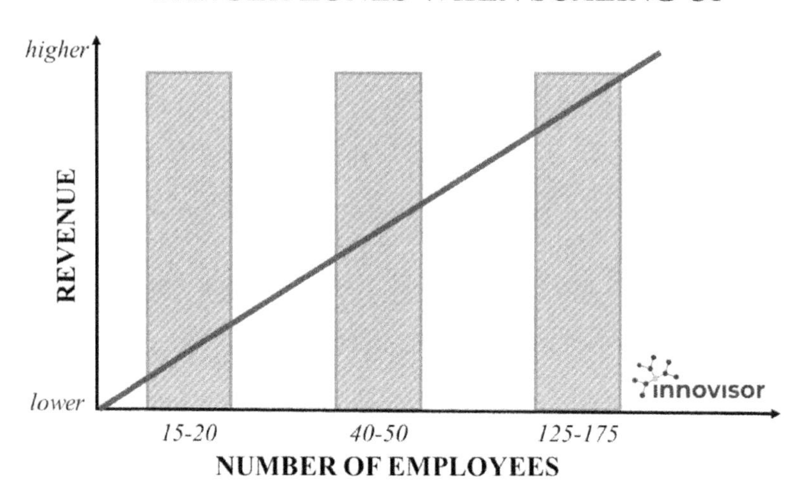

Figure 2: Danger Zones When Scaling Up

Leaders Must Take Charge to Move Through the Danger Zones

There are certain elements you need to take charge of as a leader, when moving through the danger zones. These elements include, but are not limited to:

- How do you keep your employees passionate and engaged around your purpose?
- How do you stay in sync?

- How do you organize for agility to avoid the slowness of hierarchies and silos?
- How do you sustain the customer-focus instead of getting dragged into an internal focus?
- How do you balance your need for generalists and specialists?
- And above all how do you ensure you can navigate the team connectivity through the danger zone?

Case: The Scale-Up That Almost Failed

The Swiss professional services organization has experienced rapid revenue growth, added an extra location outside the headquarters in Zürich, and had just received its first external recognition.

It was successful on all normal parameters. What started out as a small partner lead consulting company, scaled fast as they proved their capabilities and credibility with their clients. In the process, they added extra locations – a two hours commute away from their main office in Zürich – but closer to two new key clients, which they anticipated having long-term relationships with. They totaled 26 people, including four full-time freelancers.

Everything looked positive, but when you scratched below the surface a different story emerged.

While the partners had started the company as a strong and united team, it was when they grew, the problems emerged. They were too busy to be involved in delivery to clients – and often ignored the necessity for aligning expectations amongst them.

Sometimes decisions were taken too late or based on limited information. Mostly the partner meetings were cancelled.

Some of the organizational structural practices they had instilled were:

- Develop individual incentive schemes – also at partner level - focused on sales and billing.
- Outsource all support processes and build internal procedures to ensure their workability.
- Establish delivery functions with strong separate identities to drive specialization.
- Engage freelancers to fill the empty delivery slots.
- Ignore onboarding processes, so the new people can deliver projects faster.

But the mood in the office was not as good as it used to be.

Important well-liked and popular colleagues (also among clients) were resigning for other opportunities. The struggle to sell enough project services to keep scaling – or even to just maintain – became an issue leading to outspoken conflicts amongst the partners. Client Satisfaction scores started to decline. The partners all had different views of what was going on in the organization.

One partner that had mostly stayed silent and observed recommended that they gather some evidence instead of just acting on their different gut feelings.

This is where Innovisor stepped in.

The objective was to understand how the culture was being lived out. How happy people were. How they collaborated and shared knowledge with each other. If the organization was acting as ONE. How agile it was compared to its competitors.

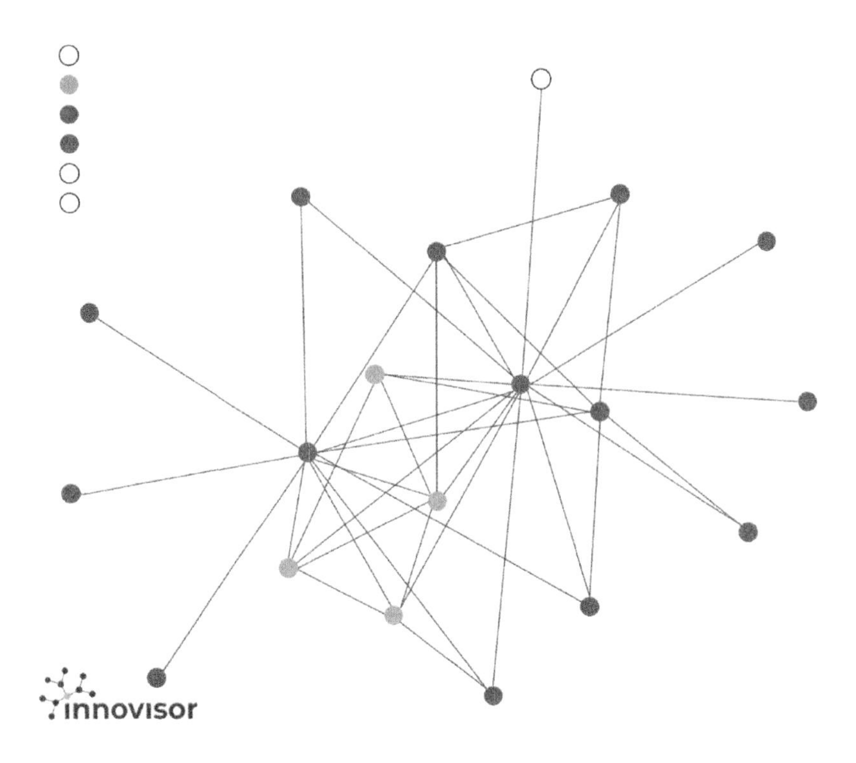

Network visual 1: Fragmented team with loosely attached group of individuals.

Things were not looking good. The organization was a loosely attached group of individuals – not working together. They did not know the competencies of each other, or even feel they had access to each other. “He will probably not help, if I ask him!” Motivation was very low – and the risk of certain key individuals leaving was very high.

The need for change was evident to all four partners.

Here is what they decided to:

- Set joint goals for improvement.

- Engage key employees as sounding board in all activities.
- Re-establish team-based incentive structures.
- Acknowledge the need for a shared identity at the organizational level – not at team or location level. Focus all social activities at this level to create ONE culture.
- Formalize informal onboarding process to make sure people knew the competencies of each other and where to ask for help.
- Formalize the People & Culture responsibility.

One year later it was a happier, more coherent, and better performing organization. Stress levels were down, and client satisfaction was up. The organization had returned to a healthier organizational growth and retained its status as a scale-up.

Growth Is Just One Barrier to Connectivity

The extensive focus on growth in organizations is just one driver of fragmentation. The world has also changed dramatically over the last 15 years. A development we in Innovisor have been to follow and track through our work with organizational networks.

In 2005, about 10% of connectivity took place outside the own team of people. However, that quickly changed dramatically with new communications infrastructures, accelerated globalization, as well as new organizational models becoming increasingly popular – a matrix organization in a matrix organization was what some leaders described to me.

As a result, in 2015, 90% of white-collar workers reported to CEB (now owned by Gartner) that most of their connectivity took place within their own team of people. Leadership remained unchanged; nevertheless, teams were still required to devise business plans confined to their respective areas on the organizational chart, leaving the majority—90%—largely without guidance.

Some leading organizations, like Roche Pharmaceuticals, started to design network-centric organizations as an answer. General Stanley McChrystal recommended the establishment of 'Teams of Teams' to forge connections across.

Cross-connectivity.

Then in 2020, the world got hit by a pandemic. In the Innovisor benchmark data, we could immediately see an impact on connectivity as it dropped by 30%. People stayed connected to their close connections, but the more distant connections were forgotten.

Regretfully, this also meant that some people got totally forgotten by their colleagues. Meaning nobody reached out to them for a chit-chat.

Nobody reached out to them for help and advice. Just imagine that for a moment. How lonely that would you make feel.

Today, at the end of 2023, it is still a staggering 25% of employees that are disconnected from their colleagues.

- Does it impact performance? – Certainly!
- Does it impact wellbeing? – YES!
- Does it impact engagement? – You bet!

This book will provide numerous examples of broken connectivity, often driven by leadership and HR/OD experts, and offer insights on preventative measures for the future.

It is my hope that you after reading this book will start to work on your connectivity, and that you will share your journey with me.

The book is organized thematically, so to help you focus this illustration can guide you to which chapters to prioritize.

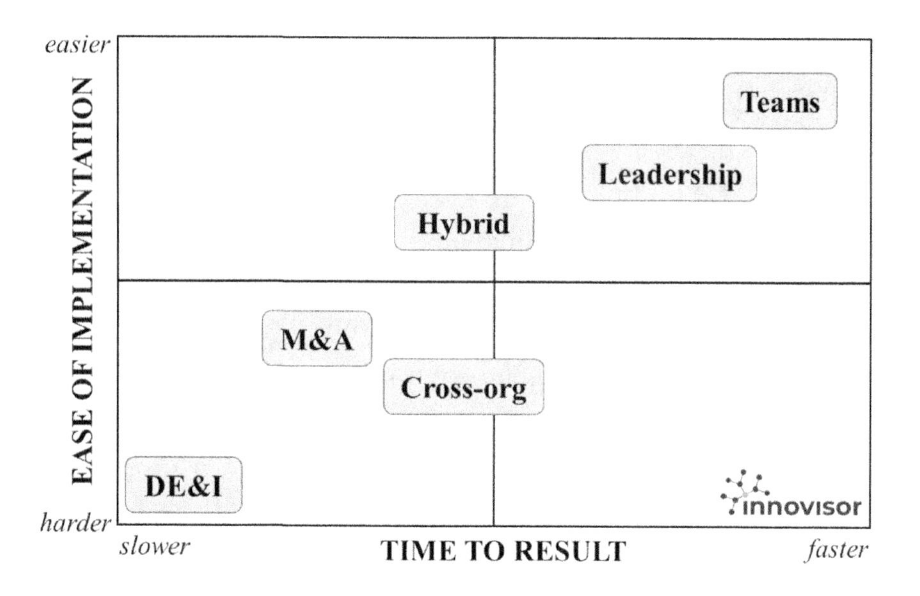

Figure 3: The themes described in part 2 of the book.

Only together can we fix the broken connectivity, and the more inspiration and experiences we share with each other, the greater the potential to transition from a handful of initial advocates to a broader connectivity movement.

Thank you in advance!

Lessons Learned & Takeaways:

Chapter 1 explores the journey of finding connectivity through a local running club in Copenhagen. This chapter highlights the impact of social connections on mental and physical health, longevity, and recovery from emergencies, setting the stage for the book's exploration of broken connectivity in society and organizations.

1. **Connectivity Peaks, Then Declines:**

   High connectivity initially boosts performance but collapses due to organizational complexities and neglect of people's needs, highlighting the critical role of sustained connectivity efforts.

2. **Dunbar's Limit: 150 Connections**

   Robin Dunbar's research reveals our brains cap meaningful connections at 150, emphasizing the importance of aligning organizational structures with this natural limit for effective cohesion.

3. **Growth Challenges Connectivity:**

   Organizational growth introduces danger zones at 15-20, 40-50, and 125-175 people, hindering connectivity. Leaders must navigate these zones by prioritizing passion, synchronization, agility, and balance.

Test Your Readiness – Is Connectivity Broken in Your Organization?

Assess your growth's impact on connectivity. Is your organization able to adapt to external factors? Is there proactive leadership navigation that prioritizes connectivity? Are you in the win, worry, or woe zone?

To what extent has organizational growth impacted connectivity?	**Minimal impact** ☐	**Moderate impact** ☐	**Significant impact** ☐
How well is your organization adapting to external factors impacting connectivity, such as the pandemic?	**Effective adaptation** ☐	**Some adaptation** ☐	**Poor adaptation** ☐
To what degree do leaders navigate growth challenges actively	**Consistently** ☐	**Occasionally** ☐	**Rarely** ☐
How well do leaders prioritize connectivity for performance and well-being?	**Effectively** ☐	**Adequately** ☐	**Poorly** ☐
	Win zone	**Worry zone**	**Woe zone**

References & Further Reading to Chapter 2

- BBC (2019) Dunbar's number: Why We Can Only Maintain 150 Relationships, available on: https://www.bbc.com/future/article/20191001-dunbars-number-why-we-can-only-maintain-150-relationships

- Hebert, P. (n.d.) Dunbar's Number and The Jetson Fallacy, available on: https://www.enterpriseengagement.org/articles/content/8468125/dunbars-number-and-the-jetson-fallacy/

- McChrystal, S. (2015) *Team of Teams: New Rules of Engagement for a Complex World*, Portfolio, ISBN: 978-1591847489

- Hansgaard, J. (2019) The Danger Zones Where Your Scale-Up Fails, available on: https://www.linkedin.com/pulse/danger-zones-where-your-scale-up-fails-jeppe-vilstrup-hansgaard/

- Hansgaard, J. (2020) The Scale-Up That Almost Failed, available on: https://www.innovisor.com/2020/10/06/the-scale-up-that-almost-failed/

- Innovisor (2019) Decision Making At the Core To Scale up As Organization, available on: https://www.innovisor.com/2019/11/27/from-being-a-start-up-to-a-scale-up/

CHAPTER THREE SO, YOU WANT TO MEND CONNECTIVITY: *THE HOW-TO GUIDE*

"If you only have a hammer, you tend to see every problem as a nail..."

– Abraham Maslow

Chapter 3: So, You Want to Mend Connectivity – The How-to Guide

In the next chapter, I will lead you through different opportunities of actionable strategies to deal with broken connectivity within and between organizations, teams, and ecosystems.

These opportunities, organized by theme, empower you to take targeted action based on your specific goals and preferences.

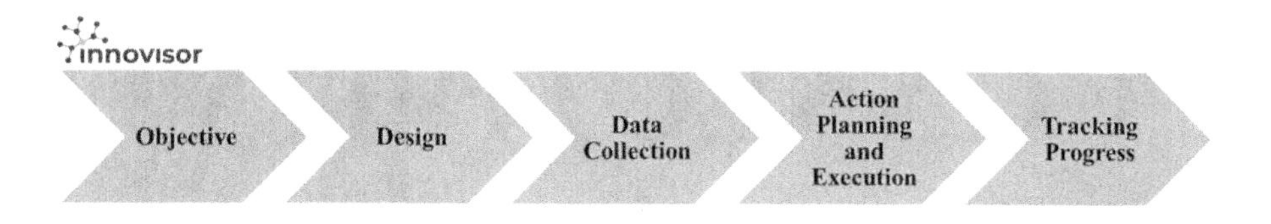

Figure 4: Innovisor Process for Improving Connectivity

Before the chapters, let's look at the five-step process we employ in Innovisor, when we are working to improve connectivity.

Step 1 - Objective

Many organizations that seek to improve connectivity often fall into the very pitfall cautioned by Maslow in his famous quote: "If you only have a hammer, you tend to see every problem as a nail."

The vital principle for you, when you want to improve connectivity must – and I emphasize – ALWAYS start with the objective.

Even if your in-house IT organization or People Analytics function insist that their recent software acquisition can fulfill all your needs for mapping connectivity, it is imperative to slow them down and establish what you want to know first.

If you are trying to discover how your people connect to each other for critical insights and knowledge outside the daily transactional processes, such as email, calendar invitations and enterprise social networks, then you need to stop them right away!

Let me share some real-life examples why I feel so strongly about this:

- A professional services company believed their Slack communities were the primary hubs for people to connect when seeking assistance. They did not. They talked to colleagues whose expertise they had learned to trust over time through many different joint assignments – a form of what some might refer to as word-of-mouth.

- A pharmaceutical company had identified individuals as most connected based on email and chat data analysis performed within Viva. It turned out that there was no overlap between them and those were reach out to in the wisdom of the crowd.

- A life science company, with the assistance of a Big 4 consulting company, concluded that their talent identification process was effective based on a high correlation between individuals on the talent list and those who sent and received the most emails.

So, ask yourself these questions:

- Why is connectivity important for both you and your organization? - What hypotheses do you aim to assess?

- What does a successful connectivity outcome look to you, and how do you plan to leverage it in your organization? - In what ways will it enhance your overall connectivity?

- Why should your people care about connectivity? What is in it for them?

- What are your success criteria? Personally, I like to use the FAST goals. Goals that are Frequent, Ambitious, Specific, and Transparent

- What are the resources available to implement the insights gained from the initiative?

While you ask yourself these questions, please also consider when you need the results and the effort you are willing to put into implementation. This can help you determine the scope you should be aiming for.

Too often I face leaders that do not understand this critical balance to strike.

Step 2 – Design

When you have defined the objective, your next step is to design how you want to generate the data that can support you in achieving your objective.

Here it is important to distinguish between nice-to-have and need-to-have. You must always challenge the inclusion of the nice-to-haves. Like when someone asks you to assess a tool as part of your work.

- How can you collect data to support the objective?

- What key questions must be addressed? – Can we take action based on the answers we expect to generate?
- Are there potential answers you will NOT generate an action for? - If so, delete it!
- What assessment mechanisms align with your objective?

Three Assessment Mechanisms for Uncovering Connectivity, and Two You Should Avoid at All Cost

There are essentially three assessment mechanisms for uncovering connectivity. They work well for certain objectives – and fall short of others.

		Use for!	Do NOT use for!	Important!
Uncover connectivity by:	**Digital Traits Assessment** *"Don't confuse activity with quality"*	• To improve governance structures with calendar data. • To improve communication around day-to-day matters with teams not located together.	• To improve connectivity – do not think you can use digital information for this. • The only thing you get to see is a transaction between people. What kind of transaction it is, will be unclear. • It cannot show, who knows whose competencies, how accessible people are to each other, how much they trust each other, or who they reach out to when they face a complex issue.	Data Protection acts, such as GDPR, CCPA and PIPEDA mandate clear consent, transparency, and secure processing for digital personal data – upholding privacy and data protection standards.

		Use for!	Do NOT use for!	Important!
Uncover connectivity by:	**Snowball Assessment** *"Works well for unknown unknowns"*	• To uncover communities and ecosystems, or what we refer to as unknown unknowns, such as: 1. business development ecosystems in densely populated regions 2. ecosystems across NGO's 3. communities or shadow organizations inside large corporations	• To get to an output in a fast way as this method requires a longer time.	Your initial snowball will determine the quality, requiring a high level of rigor and precision in your data management. At Innovisor, we iterate the snowball method until 80% of the people pointed to are already known to us. On average, this required three iterations or "snowballs."

		Use for!	Do NOT use for!	Important!
Uncover connectivity by:	**Peer-to-Peer Assessment** *"Best choice for company internal connectivity"*	• To achieve measurable change, you need to know: 1. Who knows what, and how accessible is this knowledge and expertise to others? 2. Who should you connect with, and on what, to optimize connectivity for performance and wellbeing? 3. How can you create the conditions for hybrid work, DEI, M&A integration to flourish?	• To assess the transactional processes inside your company. This method is used for transformation and change.	The quality of the output depends on the right objective, design, and data collection. Long-term success requires consistent leadership support, necessitating an actionable plan and continuous progress tracking.

Besides these three main mechanisms for mapping connectivity, there are also two mechanisms you should avoid at all costs – which I have regretfully seen again and again over the past 15 years. Always with the same poor results.

Two Mechanisms to Avoid

- **Mechanism 1 – Big Brother is Watching You:** The first mechanism is in my eyes a form of surveillance. This involves employees wearing badges to track their movement in the office. From sitting in front of the computer, being in the canteen, or spending some time in the restroom. This is just a no-go! Don't do it!
- **Mechanism 2 – I Observe. Hence, I Know:** The second mechanism is when people believe, they can observe who people are connected, how well they know each other and each other's competencies. This introduces a lot of potential biases on the observer side. So, for those considering it. Avoid this approach! Don't go there! Accept your blindness.

Step 3 – Data Collection

When you have established your design and identified your mechanism for data collection, then you need to start the data collection.

Ask yourself these questions:

- What timing should you aim for to enable best possible action planning and execution? – Do consider holidays and the company annual wheel?
- How can you efficiently collect data?
- What steps should you take to ensure all critical stakeholders are informed of the data collection progress?
- When can stakeholders anticipate receiving updates on the progress you make?

Step 4 – Action Planning & Execution

A river can cut through rock if you give it enough time. Its consistent force will pave the way for the water.

The same applies to changes in connectivity. They do not happen overnight. The stickiness of who people know, who people connect to, and who people trust is high. So, changing connectivity requires careful action planning and execution.

Over the past five years, Innovisor has analyzed longitudinal change data from hundreds of change programs across industries. About half of them have worked on improving connectivity.

Almost 80% of change programs fail in the execution phase. These programs fail to sustain the ongoing leadership support needed, and they fail to retain a project team set-up that can deliver on the objectives.

Ask yourself these questions:

- How can you develop an action plan that clearly specifies who should do what, when and why?
- How can you simulate and visualize the potential impact of the actions, making it more accessible for outsiders and key stakeholders to comprehend?
- How can you ensure critical stakeholders are actively engaged and supportive of the action plan?

- How does the plan fulfill the commitments made and the objective defined?

Step 5 – Tracking Progress

Tracking the progress of your action plan is extremely important to sustain the focus of the organization. But keep it simple and nimble!

Better practice is to track fewer parameters – like five to eight metrics maximum – with high frequency.

I recommend tracking of:

- Perceptions and emotions, on a bi-monthly basis
- Connectivity, between every three months for teams and yearly or bi-yearly for organizations.

This makes it easier to communicate with key stakeholders and to sustain their focus.

Ask yourself these questions:

- How often should progress be monitored? – by whom? – when? - and how?

- How should updates be provided to sponsors to maintain and enhance their engagement?

Lessons Learned & Takeaways:

Chapter 3 focuses on the recommended process to improve connectivity inside organizations, teams, and ecosystems.

1. **Start with a Clear Objective**

   Clear objectives anchor effective connectivity strategies, preventing the "hammer-nail" trap and ensuring purposeful initiative.

2. **Choose Assessment Mechanisms Wisely**

   Align mechanisms with objectives for accurate and meaningful insights that can lead to action.

3. **Taking Action is Required for Success**

   80% fail to move forward. Set up your metrics and track them to sustain the attention of critical stakeholders.

Test Your Readiness – How to Improve Connectivity?

Embark on connectivity improvement by considering different factors such as clarifying goals, addressing privacy, and ensuring strategic alignment. Are you in the win, worry, or woe zone?

Are your connectivity goals clearly defined?	**Yes** ☐	**Partially** ☐	**No** ☐
Have you considered data privacy regulations?	**Yes** ☐	**Partially** ☐	**No** ☐
Are key stakeholders actively engaged in the process?	**Highly** ☐	**Partially** ☐	**Not at all** ☐
Have you allocated sufficient resources for the initiative?	**Adequate** ☐	**Insufficient** ☐	**Not determined** ☐
Is there a commitment to continuous progress tracking	**Yes** ☐	**Partially** ☐	**No** ☐
	Win zone	**Worry zone**	**Woe zone**

References & Further Reading to Chapter 3

- Blue, A. (2022) *Data Is Worthless Without Context*, in Forbes, 3 January 2022, available on: https://www.forbes.com/sites/forbestechcouncil/2022/01/03/data-is-worthless-without-context/

- Sull, D. & Sull, C. (2018) With Goals, FAST Beats SMART, in: MIT Sloan Review, available on: https://sloanreview.mit.edu/article/with-goals-fast-beats-smart/

CHAPTER FOUR TEAMS – *START SMALL, IT'S THE FASTEST WAY TO SHOW RESULTS*

"Great things in business are never done by one person; they're done by a team of people."

– Steve Jobs

Chapter 4: Teams – Start Small, It's The Fastest Way to Show Results

When the Amateurs Beat the Pros

In April 1987, Denmark had only one professional football team (soccer for the US readers) – Brøndby IF, from the capital city of Copenhagen. This team had achieved European success, reaching the European quarterfinals where they lost against legendary FC Porto from Lisbon, Portugal.

They were now to play against a team from five levels below. A team of local fishermen, factory workers, bookkeepers, and a TV shop assistant from the little town of Skagen, located as far away from the capital as one could get in Denmark.

"Do you want to come?"

I have five brothers, and they are all obsessed with football.

I am not! I am more into individual sports like track & field (my favorite), bicycling, and cross-country skiing (only on TV). Nevertheless, the prospect of a family trip to see the best Danish football team ever was attractive, prompting me to say yes.

I am happy I did because I learned a lesson for life.

The underrated team of amateurs triumphed over the full-time professionals, winning seven to six in a penalty shootout. This unexpected victory created the biggest sensation in the history of Danish football, proving that sometimes, the underdogs can outshine even the most established contenders.

Picture 1: The Skagen players celebrate the goalkeeper after their win (Source: Åge Sørensen on dr.dk)

Skagen has taught me that a disciplined and coherent team, working collaboratively and clearly defining their objectives, can overcome even the most daunting competitors.

In sports there are many similar examples, where great teams find motivation in each other that enables them to win. Even the great

Michael Jordan has said: “Talent wins games, but teamwork and intelligence wins championships.”

Somehow this lesson has not always transferred into the business world. Our emphasis on individuals and the romanticization of the “strong man” persist, leading to the reinforcement of behaviors that are counterproductive to teamwork and connectivity.

Black Holes and People Magnets

Most of us have worked with a magnetic person. Someone whose sheer presence energizes a room because the person so talented and likeable that we all want to be close to him or her. A person we seek out at the water cooler, at the lunch table, or whose cubicle we try pass by more than once per day. The person who is always ready to smile, listen and help! It’s pure magnetism and we just love to collaborate with such a person.

I am sure you have met such a person! I managed such a person some years ago without recognizing her magnetism. I could only see her just above average performance scores.

Not really a talent in my view.

I was SO wrong.

She was the glue.

In reality, she served as the glue holding the department together, fostering cohesion and motivating colleagues to go the extra mile for the company. Also, when it was getting tough.

On the flip side, we have all encountered the black hole in the workplace. The person that drains the energy in the room by just entering it. The black hole might be extremely competent, but the likability factor is so low that their competency is not played in the collaborative networks.

The black hole is the person that keeps looking for mistakes, that tells you again and again "this has been done before," and will visibly shows you that you are disruptive, when you ask even the smallest question.

Sometimes the black hole feels so competent that you - in his own view - should feel honored to work with him or her.

In reality, you avoid such a person. You go to lunch at a different time and pick the other end of the meeting table when he or she is in a meeting with you.

Collaboration that is supposed to take place, does not take place. Excuses for not interacting with the black hole just keep lining up.

I have also worked with a black hole. Regretfully, I was so close to him that I could not see the de-energizing impact he had on the rest of his colleagues. My personal bias was too big. In fact, I considered him and treated him as a talent.

Get the Right Evidence in Place

The magnetic person and the black hole are each other's opposites - and they are hard to identify for leaders. However, even if they are hard to identify, it does not mean it is impossible. You should do whatever you can to replace your personal biases with true insights.

In my view, you are running a very high organizational risk, by just leaving your identification of the magnetic person and the black hole to luck.

A risk that might cause your people to leave the company. The magnetic person because this person does not feel acknowledged. The colleagues of the black hole because the black hole is so de-energizing to be around that they would rather work for a different company. Imagine the impact on performance on your organization.

In both cases, organizational network analysis, now a core component of Innovisor, proved invaluable. It allowed me to see the real organization, not only the formal structures. I recognized the risk of losing the wrong person. Something that could easily result in a drop in performance we would NEVER recover from.

It enabled me to see the devastating impact a de-energizing individual had. It helped me to take informed decisions, treat the right people as talents, and execute the needed organizational changes.

It benefited me, but above all it also benefited the organization!

Friction was removed, engagement re-established, and trust in leadership skyrocketed.

Since I had that personal experience, it has been my passion to empower organizations all over the world to become a success by giving them the same insights as I received. Still, I only had case and anecdotal evidence to prove my beliefs.

Then, along came the most visionary HR Executive I have met in my life.

PharmaCo Proves the Value of Coherent Teams

We were running an analysis of networks for one of the most successful pharma companies. Apart from our standard deliverables, the HR Executive had a few extra assignments for us.

He had a hypothesis that he wanted us to confirm.

He believed strongly that the better-connected sales teams were outside their own team, the better they would be performing.

He gave us access to performance data of about 800 sales teams with between 20-30 employees each. We were eager to start crunching.

Regretfully, we could not confirm his hypothesis. Being well-connected outside did not make you perform better. Cross-organizational connectivity is in essence not about everybody being connected outside – it is about the right people being connected outside.

The HR Executive was visibly disappointed.

The performance data, however, allowed us to check one of my own lifelong hypotheses. Would the connected team perform better?

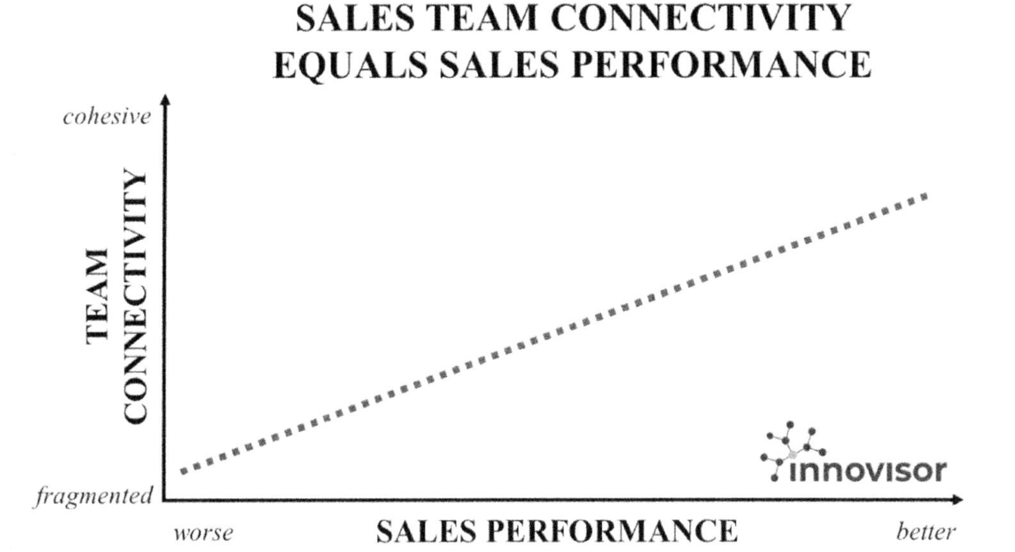

Figure 6: Sales Team Connectivity Equals Sales Performance

Yes, it did. The data was 100% clear. The connected team always performed better.

We have since seen the exact same results in not only other pharma organizations, but also in professional services, insurance, and manufacturing. For the HR Executive, it was the lightbulb moment of his life.

He ended up skipping their individual performance management system in favor of a team focused performance management system. Colquitt (2017) ended up writing a book about it.

We also saw something else in the data.

Lone-Wolf Behavior Impacts Team Performance

I am sure you have met a “lone wolf.” Especially if you have had anything to do with sales. A lone wolf is sometimes described with the words "he is exceeding quota, so we just let him do what he wants to do."

The “lone wolf” is a taker to use the terminology of Grant (2013) in his brilliant book Give & Take. The “lone wolf” follows instincts. The “lone wolf” is self-assured. The “lone wolf” is difficult to control. And often the “lone wolf” is a high performer within sales.

That all sounds good… right?

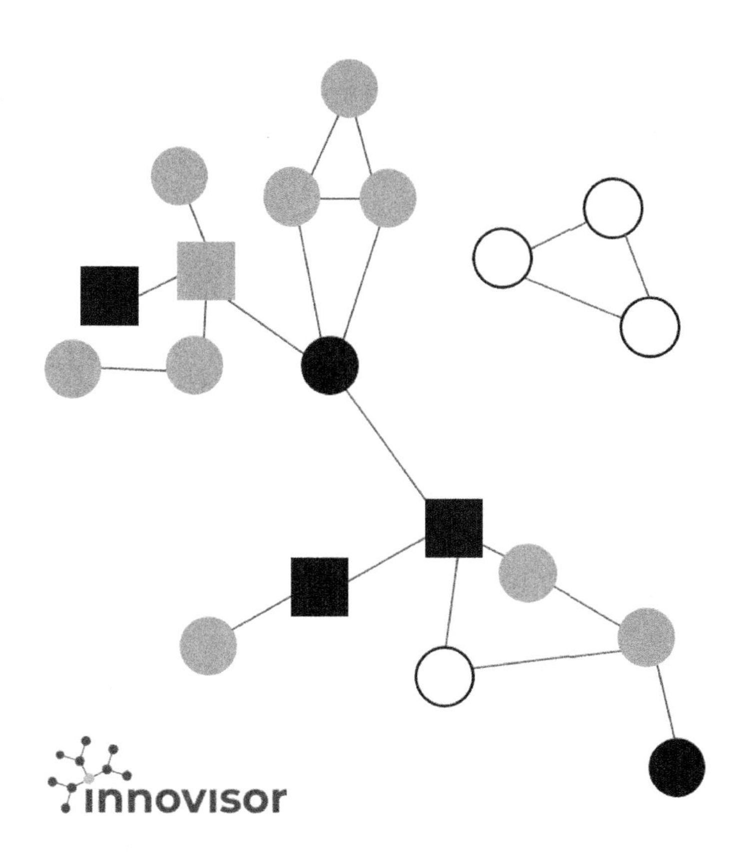

Network visual 2: Connectivity network of a low-performing team

No, because the behavior of a “lone wolf” has an impact on the team.

The behavior is dragging the performance of its colleagues down. The “lone wolf” might be the best, when you assess the individual numbers, but the team suffers. So far, many sales directors have accepted the “lone wolf” because of the individual performance, but they should not! The connectivity of your sales teams has a direct impact on sales performance.

Similarly, we proved the value of connectivity on performance in a law firm. Partners that seemed to be high performers, were in fact the lowest performers, when their performance was measured holistically. The conclusion was clear. The more the partners worked together on their clients, the more money the company earned.

In a recent case, we again discovered that the best performing sales teams were the ones with the highest connectivity. In two-thirds of the disconnected sales teams achieving higher connectivity was just a matter of connecting a few individuals.

In one case, connecting four people improved connectivity by 25%, which according to our simulations could improve sales by 30%. Their "lone wolf" behavior had led to silo-mentality and no sharing of leads across.

Case - How Facilitation Improved Team Connectivity by 40%

If we want to improve team connectivity, we need to discipline it rather than leave it to laissez faire.

We need to treat the building of team connectivity with the same care as when we host major dinner parties and want to make sure all our guests will have a good time. Where you make sure that the right people are seated next to each other, or you make sure to introduce the right people to each other.

Every single time you allocate people to a project or a task you should see it as an opportunity to build connections.

Who should be connected with whom and why?

In the same way, when you host meetings, it's crucial to carefully plan who should have one-on-one discussions, who should be seated next to each other, and who should be in what work groups. Each interaction among your team members presents an opportunity for you to facilitate connections and foster a sense of camaraderie.

Too often we ignore this opportunity and think connections will happen by themselves.

They will not!

In a 25-person team we worked in an energy company, we managed to improve team connectivity by 42% by just adding an extra layer of evidence-based facilitation to their two-day offsite.

Illustration 1 – The Power of being intentional with your 1-on-1's

- We listed 1:1's, where the participants saw a potential in connecting more with each other, but somehow always had found an excuse not to do it.
- We grouped them into 5 groups to discuss business relevant topics with the hidden agenda to create knowledge of each other's competencies and sympathy for each other. The latter accelerated by small games.
- We seated them, so they were forced to chitchat with someone they did not know beforehand, and again made sure to get the conversation started with a few conversation starters.

Yes, such actions might create friction in the interactions, but as long there is alignment on the objective this is justifiable.

Simple actions. Huge impact!

Final Remarks

My final remark for you is a quote from Peter Senge:

> **"Contrary to popular myth, great teams are not characterized by an absence of conflict. On the contrary, one of the most reliable indicators of a team that is continuously learning is the visible conflict of ideas. In great teams, conflict becomes productive!"**

Lessons Learned & Takeaways:

Chapter 4 illustrates the potency of teamwork over individual talent. When looking into teams, this is also where you can find organizational success. When you emphasize the workplace dynamics of "magnetism" and "black holes," you will be able to showcase the impact of cohesive teams and strategic connectivity.

1. **Teamwork Triumphs Over Individual Talent**

   Skagen's amateur team showcased the power of cohesive goals. Unlike sports, business often favors individuals. Michael Jordan's wisdom echoes—talent wins games, but it's teamwork and intelligence that secure championships, a principle underappreciated in the corporate world.

2. **Identify Impactful Individuals**

   The workplace mirrors magnetism and black holes—recognizing the glue individuals, vital for team cohesion, is essential. Diagnostics uncover organizational risks. Overlooking the de-energizing impact of "black holes" risks talent loss and hinders performance. Strategic recognition and elimination of drainers foster engagement and trust.

3. **Connectivity Enhances Team Performance**

   "Lone wolves" in sales may excel individually, but their behavior drags down the team. Connectivity emerges as a key factor in sales, law firms, and beyond. Purposeful facilitation, acknowledging every interaction as an opportunity to build connections, becomes imperative. Ignoring this, organizations risk stagnation and underperformance.

Test Your Readiness – Are You Able to Start Small?

Are you ready to start small with a diagnostic on your team's connectivity? Answer the below questions and find out where most of the answers fall in. Are you in the win, worry, or woe zone?

To what extent do you believe in the power of teamwork over individual talent in achieving success?	**Favor teamwork** ☐	**Neutral** ☐	**Favor individual** ☐
In your opinion, is your organization more inclined to celebrate individual achievements or cohesive teamwork?	**Cohesive teamwork** ☐	**Balanced emphasis** ☐	**Individual achievements** ☐
To what extent do you think lone wolf behavior affects team performance in your work environment?	**Significant** ☐	**Moderate** ☐	**Negligible** ☐
How intentional is your organization in facilitating and promoting team connectivity during work-related interactions	**High** ☐	**Moderate** ☐	**Limited** ☐
To what extent does your organization prioritize strategic connections when assigning people to projects or tasks?	**High priority** ☐	**Moderate priority** ☐	**Low priority** ☐
Does your organization tend to leave the building of team connectivity to chance rather than international efforts?	**Mostly intentional** ☐	**Mixed approach** ☐	**Mostly left to chance** ☐
	Win zone	**Worry zone**	**Woe zone**

References & Further Reading to Chapter 4

- Colquitt, A. (2017) *Next Generation Performance Management: The Triumph of Science Over Myth and Superstition*, Information Age Publishing, ISBN: 978-1681239323

- Corporate Executive Board (2015) Are Lone Wolf Sales Reps Right for Your Organization, available on: https://www.cebglobal.com/blogs/are-lone-wolf-sales-reps-right-for-your-organization-2/

- Gardner, H. (2015) Why It Pays to Collaborate With Your Colleagues, in: The American Lawyer, available on: https://www.law.com/americanlawyer/almID/1202718495533/

- Grant, A. (2013) *Give and Take: Why Helping Other Drives Our Success*, Penguin Books, ISBN: 978-0315782143

- Grant, A. (2014) The Top Ten Signs You Might Be a Taker, available on: https://www.linkedin.com/pulse/20140320115939-69244073-the-top-ten-signs-you-might-be-a-taker/

- Hansgaard, J. (2015) Where is The Black Hole in Your Organization, available on: https://www.linkedin.com/pulse/where-black-hole-your-organization-jeppe-vilstrup-hansgaard/

- Hansen, M.T. (2009) *Collaboration: How Leaders Avoid the Traps, Build Common Ground, and Reap Big Results*, Harvard Business Review Press, ISBN: 978-1422115152

CHAPTER FIVE LEADERSHIP – *YOUR MOST DISCONNECTED TEAM*

"Building a cohesive leadership team is the first critical step that an organization must take if it is to have the best chance at success."

– Patrick Lencioni

Chapter 5: Leadership – Your Most Disconnected Team

Disconnected Leadership Teams Is the Rule

Over the years, I have had the privilege to help leadership teams become more united, to work as one, to walk in the same direction.

One team stands out clearly in my memory – *to help them was a side task, from another side task* – to map its shadow organizations. It was a functional leadership team in a global pharmaceutical company.

It quickly became evident to me that the leadership team was not seen as a *team* by their people. You did not have to spend many moments in the canteen to know that. So, in a session with one of the leaders I queried a bit about their one-year business plan.

He happily shared everything about the three key projects he owned, but when asked him about the projects of the other leaders, and how they were all connected, he was clueless.

"I don't know, and I don't care!"

This shocked me. I went straight to the top leader to the discuss, how we could turn his leadership team of 11 disconnected individuals into ONE team. My proposal was approved. I started by generating the facts.

If You Want Long-Term Success, Cortisol Beats Dopamine

In a situation like this, many leaders go straight into firefighting mode. They want to solve the issue quickly, so they call for a meeting, an offsite, or hire an outside consultant.

This satisfies their dopamine craving. However, the better choice would be to first pause, and then diagnose what the right approach is. An approach driven by cortisol.

Only the best leaders do the latter. Luckily this leader was one of them.

In the next two weeks, I had a series of semi-structured interviews with each leader collecting insights on how well the leaders knew the reasoning behind the strategy and the direction they were supposed to take.

It was clear they were not on the same planet. They did not agree on their current position. Some thought they were doing excellently and that they should continue as is. Others said that they needed to change every single work practice they had, to not risk being outsourced.

Nobody – *literally 0%* – knew the key projects of their colleagues in the leadership team. Some could not even name their own key projects.

I presented the evidence from the interviews in the next leadership meeting. It had mandatory participation. Normally, only about half of the leaders showed up.

The evidence was so clear. Everybody could see the need for change.

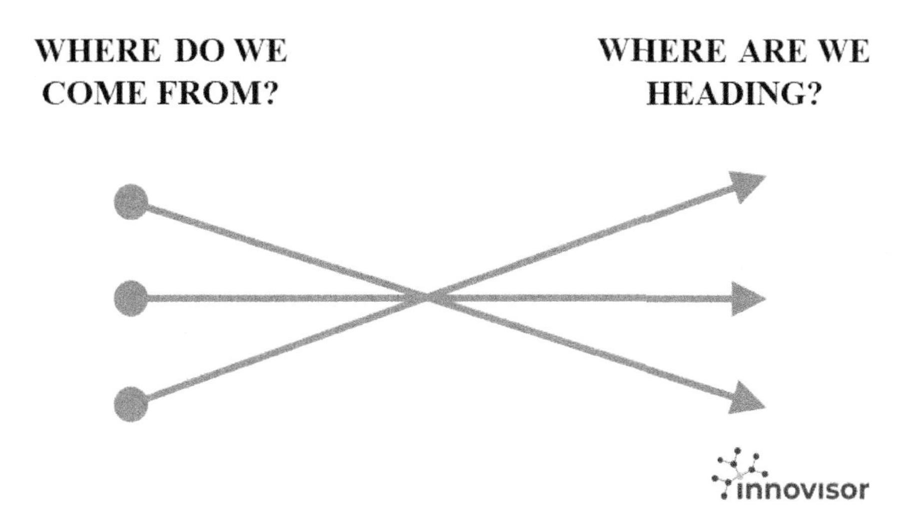

Illustration 2: Leadership teams are the most disconnected teams.

How often have you heard leaders say, “we need to break down the silos” and then shortly after the leaders launch collaboration activities with the objective to bust silos.

The only common denominator of all the activities being that they have an impact on everybody else in their organizations.

Not the looking internally at the leaders themselves…

Huge Investments Go into Leadership Teams

Leadership teams are consistently the teams that organizations invest the most money in. In leadership off-sites, in personality assessments for leaders, in individual leadership training and development, in social events for leaders, and so forth. Somehow, all these practices don't pay off.

They scratch the surface, but do not get the root cause of the issue. Despite the huge investments in leadership teams, they are still by far the worst connected teams.

Leaders still pull in different directions according to their own preferences, they compete for internal resources rather than thinking about the greater objective, they send mixed signals to the employees rather than stand as ONE and they compete against each other to position themselves for the next level.

As a good friend once said to me:

"It is always sad when getting a bigger slice of the cake becomes more important than baking a bigger cake!"

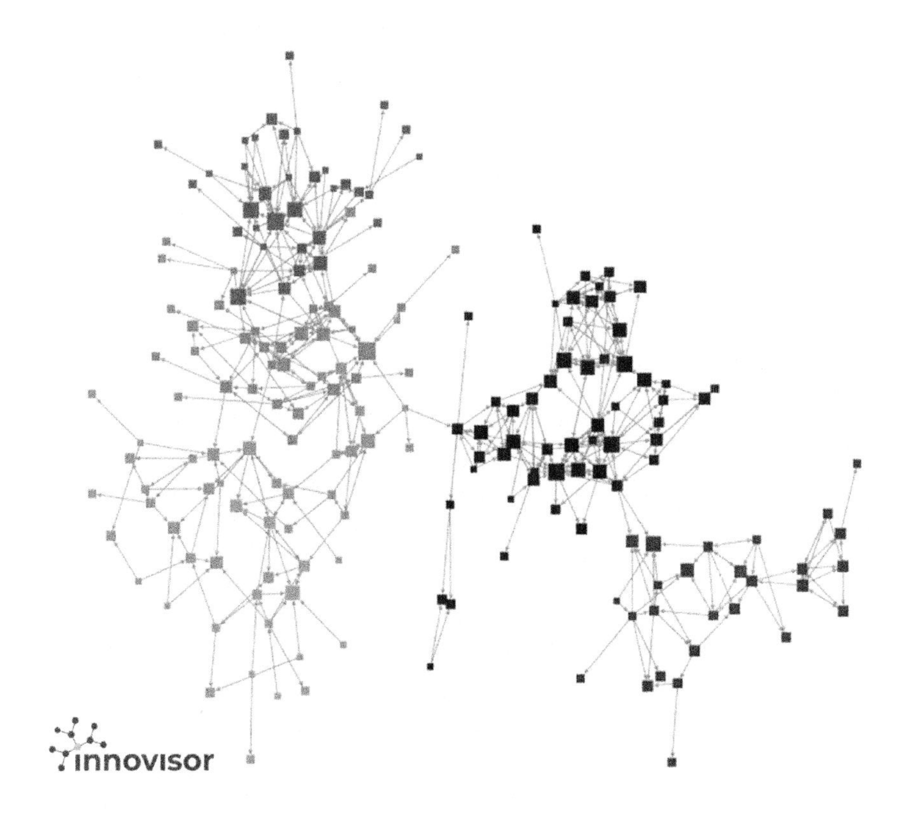

Network visual 3: Connectivity within 150-person leadership team

Often leaders simply dislike each other. They just do not say it out loud. The result is fragmentation and silos. In Innovisor's work, we discover this again and again.

In reality, leadership teams struggle more than any other team when it comes to effective communication and connections. On average, they are 20% less connected than other teams according to the Innovisor benchmark database.

In one case, the leadership team of a rapidly growing scale-up physically shared an office, but despite their proximity, the team did not connect. The leadership team, which had engaged Innovisor to foster unity throughout the organization, faced a paradox—they struggled to connect within their own six-member team. The repercussions were not confined to the leadership level; the entire organization felt the impact. This highlighted a crucial necessity for a unified and cohesive leadership team capable of providing clear guidance to steer the entire operation.

Lead by Example to Bust Silos

If we want to bust silos, we need the leadership teams to quit talking about what their employees are failing at connecting around, and instead start to lead by example, such as by busting their own silos.

We see repeatedly that leaders point to colleagues in the leadership team that could make them more effective if they could collaborate more with them. Still, they do not make a connection to their colleague.

The basic action of reaching out and asking for help does not happen. Maybe because it is too vulnerable or too embarrassing to ask for help? Maybe because it leaves the leader exposed when the leaders fight for the top position in the leadership team?

Lack of Leadership Cohesion Is a Change Blocker

Innovisor has studied and analyzed patterns, signals, activities, and interventions in our change data collected from clients of all company sizes and industries across 70+ different countries, since our inception.

In this work, we identified "Six Change Blockers" that you must combat to win your change.

One of them is "Leadership Cohesion," so the ability of the leadership team to work as one. Rather than having a constant tug-of-war.

Illustration 2: Tug of war (Source: Michael Rothschild on LinkedIn)

This means that the cohesion of your leadership team has a direct impact on your ability to succeed with change. With Gartner predicting in 2023 that every single company will face more than three firm-wide change programs per year until 2026, connecting your leadership team must be your highest priority.

Status quo is not an option.

What To Do to Fix Leadership Disconnectivity?

So, what can be done to fight the silos in the leadership teams? Essentially, the top leader needs to take on the responsibility to make it happen.

Responsibility cannot be delegated.

- Leaders are 4 x times more likely to connect to leaders at their own level, than people one level above or below.
- Leaders have close to 0% interaction with people two levels below themselves in the hierarchy.
- 80% of leadership teams are not working as ONE.

Source: Innovisor Benchmark Database

So, what can you do. Again, the first step is to bring in the facts, and run your analysis of the connectivity. Check who is not connecting to whom? – and who should connect? Set your connectivity goals and make them visible.

From there on you need to.

1. **Discipline Connectivity:** Force those leaders who fail to connect into those uncomfortable one-on-one conversations and ask them for a plan. If they cannot bury their silo thinking and come up with a credible plan, then find new members for the leadership team.
2. **Ensure Alignment:** If the leadership team is not aligned in the strategic direction, then the employees are never going to follow suit. Make sure the leaders communicate and role model the same direction and priorities.

The Global Engineering Leadership Team That Met, but Never Connected

The leadership team of a global engineering organization met every month for two days – except in the months of July and December. Every time they spent the first day on team building activities, which typically due to the personal interests of CEO involved some physical challenges.

They covered 80 kilometers by mountain bikes, hiked to the top of mountains, engaged in kayaking, and even jumped out of helicopters into water, among other activities. The CEO really wanted to create a coherent and high performing team.

Somehow, the CHRO – the only woman in the group of 13 executives – did not feel they had succeeded. Not least as, three years before, they had acquired another engineering company with strong representation in China and in Central Europe.

Among the 13 executives, eight shared a common mother tongue, and it was not English. Conversely, the remaining five executives had distinct languages as their mother tongues. During social conversations in the breaks, the group of eight executives who shared the same language tended to switch to that language, unintentionally excluding the other five executives.

The most recent client satisfaction research also stated that the clients did not feel they were contracting with a global engineering company with access to global expertise and experience. It felt rather like contracting with a local engineering company.

The CHRO had invited me and Innovisor to help improve connectivity during a workshop on the second day of their leadership meeting.

The second day of the leadership meeting was always spent on updates from the CIO, CFO, CHRO and CEO on progress made with the corporate initiatives in the strategy. The leaders of the regions – North America, South America, North Europe, Central Europe, South Europe, Asia, and Australia listened, took notes and to some extent nurtured their hangovers.

This time, guided by a connectivity analysis, we implemented the following strategies for their second day of the leadership meeting:

- We reorganized their seating arrangements.
- We grouped them into what felt like uncomfortable groups.
- We forced them into one-on-ones, such as pairing the regional leaders from Asia and North America, allowing them to spend valuable time on discussing a shared key client. Something they both pointed to as being valuable, but somehow never had come around to discuss.
- We helped them to focus on conversation that they group had yet to engage in collectively:
    - How can we as a group work together to achieve our goals?
    - How can we make each other more effective?
    - What should we stop doing to create time for prioritizing these activities?

The difference was felt immediately. Suddenly they started to talk about "we" rather than "I." The results included a bi-weekly meeting amongst the regional leaders without the involvement of headquarters to discuss key clients. Shortly after, another meeting was added to align around global tenders. Lastly, the one-on-ones conversations accelerated.

No one was ever again more than a phone call away.

Final Remarks

Disconnected leadership teams are the rule.

It happens very rarely that we experience leadership teams that work well together as one. In our research related to six change blockers, we learned that about 80% of leadership teams fail to work as one. There is always an internal tug-of-war going on.

We also learned that with the right intentional activities the leadership team can work as one, and then there is no limit to what can be achieved.

Lessons Learned & Takeaways:

Chapter 5 explores the common challenge of disconnected leadership teams. This common challenge of the importance of unity and direction is shown through a real-life example from a pharmaceutical company – underlining the need for proactive leadership to address this issue.

1. **Disconnected Leadership Teams Are Common**

   Many leadership teams operate independently, hindering success. Collaboration and shared direction are often lacking, which is impacting overall organizational performance.

2. **Cohesive Leaderships Team Are Vital for Change**

   A unified leadership team is essential for navigating change successfully. That way you can address key obstacles and ensure a collective commitment to organizational transformation.

3. **Top Leadership Must Lead by Example**

   It requires proactive leadership to overcome leadership disconnection. The top leader's active involvement fosters unity and collaboration, setting the stage for a more cohesive and effective team.

Test Your Readiness – Are You Ready to Combat the Most Disconnected Team?

Assess the readiness of your leadership teams to combat the issue dysconnectivity. What is the leadership team's awareness of connectivity, and are the members open to change? Are you in the win, worry, or woe zone?

Are leadership team members recognizing the challenge of connectivity in their leadership team?	**Fully aware** ☐	**Somewhat** ☐	**Not at all** ☐
Is top leadership taking proactive steps to foster unity within the leadership teams?	**Very proactive** ☐	**To some extent** ☐	**Not at all** ☐
How open do you believe the leadership team members are to receiving feedback on their collaboration?	**Open** ☐	**Neutral** ☐	**Resistant** ☐
Do you believe leadership team members take personal responsibility for improving team cohesion?	**Always** ☐	**Occasionally** ☐	**Rarely** ☐
	Win zone	**Worry zone**	**Woe zone**

References & Further Reading to Chapter 5

- Innovisor (2018) From Misaligned Management to Realizing Full Potential, available on: https://www.innovisor.com/2018/04/18/from-misaligned-management-to-realizing-full-potential/

- Innovisor (2018) From Untapped Potentials to Effective Leadership Summit, available on: https://www.innovisor.com/2018/10/24/from-untapped-potentials-to-effective-leadership-summit/

CHAPTER SIX CROSS-ORGANIZATIONAL – *SUSTAIN YOUR SILOS, BE A SPEEDBOAT*

"The real killer of productivity is a lack of connection."

– Mervyn Dinnen

Chapter 6: Cross-Organizational – Sustain Your Silos, Be a Speedboat

"What matters is only the local!"

I was conducting one of many interviews for this book and could easily hear the frustration.

75+ affiliates in the same company, but almost organized in a franchise structure with accountability limited by borders. Each affiliate sells the exact same products and with a high degree of autonomy on how to do it.

The model had worked well for decades, and the resistance to change from the local leaders was remarkable. Changing the current siloed way of working would challenge their high-profile positions. Any initiative pursuing cross-organizational developments and innovations was blocked.

But times were changing. Business was changing. Technology was changing.

- Customers were now more connected to customers from other countries.

- Customers had easier access to previously restricted or inaccessible product information.
- Social Media Influencers with global followership had revolutionized news flows via X/Twitter, TikTok, Instagram, and YouTube.
- Access to local skills was challenged by changing work habits.

So, despite the stark resistance from the leaders, the approval to pursue enhanced cross-organizational connections was finally achieved.

"Break down the organizational silos."

First a Few Facts

In Innovisor, we have collected data on how organizations, functions and teams connect to each other for years. People always primarily work with people of their own kind. How much they work with and should work with their own kind, depends on what they deliver to the organization.

- Support organizations like HR, Finance, and IT should expect to use a maximum of 50-60% of their connectivity on connecting with themselves. In the Innovisor benchmark data HR lies at 55%, Finance at 58%, and IT at 67% at the time of writing.

- A core organization like Production should use a minimum of 80% of their connectivity on connecting with themselves in Production. In the Innovisor benchmark data, they are at 86% at the time of writing.

The question always is what about the remaining percentages. Who should connect to whom outside.

Like in the HR organization of a Middel Eastern oil company, where internal connections accounted for 55% of their interactions. The important question was around where they spent the remaining 45% of their time. Is it spent on those functions that needs help with e.g. massive recruitment efforts, or is it spent on the friendly Finance people sitting on the same floor in the tall building that you co-incidentally also connect to outside of work.

Regretfully it was the latter.

Cross-Organizational Connectivity Is Not About Breaking Down the Silos

I have heard the phrase "we must break down the silos" so many times that I have lost count.

It is an expression that has snuck into the business language without anyone thinking through its meaning and consequences. A favorite saying of executives across the globe. Collaboration technology companies love it too. Don't get me started on those.

Silos are, however, much better than their reputation. They add closeness and trust to our working lives. A place where we can be ourselves and do not have to pretend! Above all, silos fulfill our desire for a sense of belonging. So, I say:

"Save the silos! They are your secret weapon."

A weapon our competitors cannot copy. A weapon that can transform our businesses into agile "speed boats," particularly in an ever-evolving business landscape.

Silos are the most efficient way to organize work. They are much more agile to navigate and easier to transform than any other organizational structure – all while preserving valuable social capital. Additionally, silos have the added benefit that the members of the silo have a sense of belonging and are more likely to help each other when needed.

What is not to like?

I believe it is about time we start to praise silos for all the good they do!

Cross-Organizational Innovation Without Busting the Silos

Silos are the most efficient and agile way to organize work, but they lack certain capabilities that we require to win in business. Particularly, innovation and development.

But there is a way to innovate without busting your silos! You just need to connect the silos in the right places, with the right people.

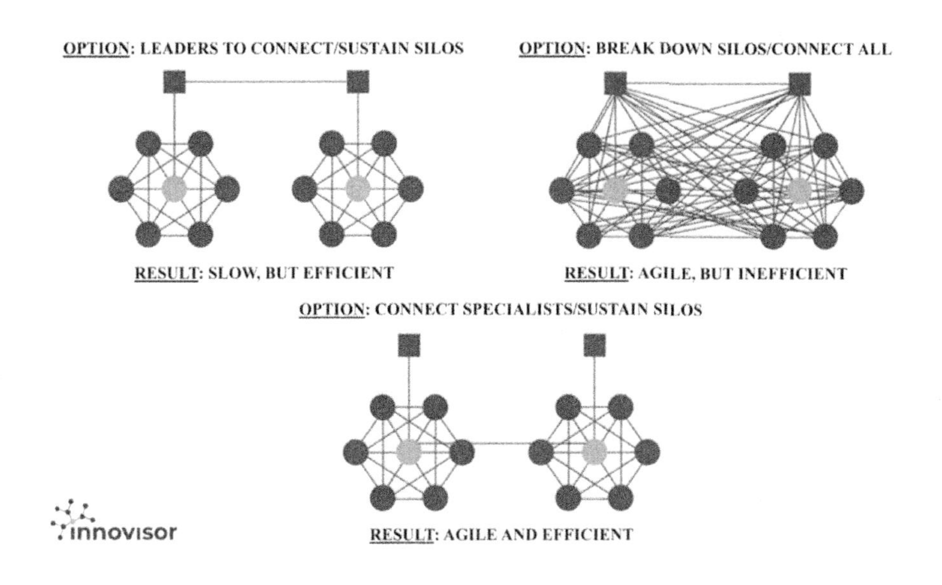

Illustration 3: Different connectivity approaches with different outcomes

A Leadership Task Treated with a Laissez-Faire Approach

Connecting the silos in the right places with the right people is a leadership task. All too often treated with a laissez-faire approach.

Who should connect about what, when and why? But what are the right places? – and who are the right people?

First, we need to understand the problem with the current approaches.

The problem with "let's break down the silos!"

When a Senior Executive says, "let's break down the silos," then one of two things typically happens.

Both have the same result: Inefficiency and lack of trust in leadership.

- **You Let Employees Solve It**: You leave it to employees to figure out who they should connect with, and they start to have coffee conversations, informal touch bases, invite numerous people into projects, coordination meetings become longer with more participants and decisions slow down. Widespread inefficiency.

- **You Invest in Collaboration Technology:** You implement a collaboration technology tool and believe you have fixed the problem… but then the 1/9/90 rule sets in, and nothing happens. 1% of your employees use your tool, 9% listen in, and 90% are disconnected from it. Wasted investment!

These approaches to creating more connectivity make employees lose faith in their leaderships ability to lead.

"Super tanker" versus "speed boat" – What do you want to be?

The illustration shows what is often desired when people talk about breaking down silos.

The result looks intriguing when displayed from a network perspective.

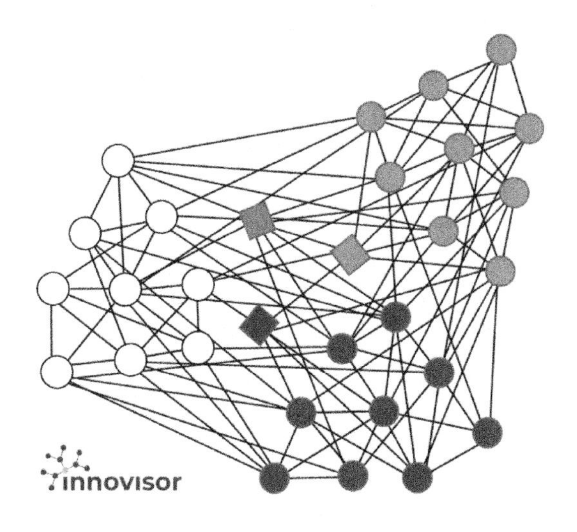

Network visual 3: The dangers when everybody is connected to everybody.

Everybody is connected to everybody, and widespread collaboration and knowledge sharing can take place, but the risks are evident:

- Collaboration overload.
- Employees not knowing who to reach out to, when they need help.
- Bureaucracy and meeting hell.

What was initially implemented to enhance agility can quickly transform into a cumbersome and slow organization, where every decision requires extensive coordination and input, resembling a "super tanker."

There is a different way, and it requires us to stop breaking down the silos. Instead, we should save them and use the obvious strengths the silos possess to build organizations that are efficient and agile. Where people know and trust each other, and where they have a sense of belonging. They are your "speedboats!"

The value and comfort of being an organizational super tanker in the hyper-competitive and dynamic business environment of today is questionable.

The size of the "super tanker" has become a challenge. Sudden icebergs in the form of business model and technology disruptions pop up everywhere without leaving the organizations sufficient time to maneuver around them.

Maneuverability is not the only challenge! The "super tankers" are also challenged by their ability to innovate and to engage employees.

This is where the silos in your organization can help! You should save the silos and the obvious advantages they have. And then turn them into an army of inter-connected "speed boats."

But how, you might ask.

The Three Steps to an Army of "Speed Boats"

Here are three steps that will give you ENGAGEMENT, ALIGNMENT, and INNOVATION. Three critical organizational ingredients that most organizations struggle with delivering on:

Step 1 - Save the Silos

Skip the corporate "breaking down the silos" lingo. Silos are a fact of life in the way people relate to each other. Instead, you should save them and empower them to act! This is where you drive ENGAGEMENT for your employees. In close relationships with likeminded people, and it is an extremely efficient way of organizing.

Step 2 – Build an Army of "Speed Boats"

Work with your leadership group. Make sure they act as ONE coherent team. They must buy-in to the overall strategic direction, values, and principles – and then have the power to drive their own "speed boats" forward without too much supervision from the overall leadership. This is where the critical ALIGNMENT happens.

Step 3: Connect the Right People Across the Silos

Identify the right specialists and go-to people in the silos and orchestrate their interaction and connectivity across the silos to achieve innovation and breakthrough thinking. To connect what was previously divided. To connect us with them. To explore what is on the other side. To find new opportunities. To establish a short cut. To support INNOVATION.

Remember it is only about 5% of the employees, or less, that should connect across the silos. They need sufficient time and resources to build critical connections that will allow them also to have value-adding conflicts in their interactions.

And it is not leaders that are to be connected! This is where you drive the innovation that will help you survive.

Language and Other Barriers

Back to the interview. Barriers for connecting with each other. Language was an issue across 75+ countries. Very few spoke the company language of English as their mother tongue; this created a barrier for inclusion in the organizational networks, primarily driven by self-exclusion.

Human Connection Improves Quality by Ten Times

Armed with a peer-to-peer based organizational network analysis delivered by Innovisor, they knew exactly who to connect with each other.

At first, the idea was to connect them to work related tasks, objectives, and teams by creating visibility of people's past experiences and skills – almost like a CV database – but it was soon evident something else was needed to connect people. The human connection. And the trust generated from knowing each other from a maybe unrelated activity in the past.

Using the human connection and trust as the driver enabled them to improve quality of cross-organizational connectivity by ten times.

Case: Cross-Organizational Centers of Expertise

A 13,000 people technology organization needed to focus efforts within seven cores areas, such as Artificial Intelligence, Enterprise Architecture, and Cloud Computing. They had already identified the people they wanted to head up the centers of expertise in their headquarters, a top-down identification of experts.

At Innovisor, we understand that relying solely on individual judgment often falls short. Instead, we advocate for tapping into the collective wisdom of the crowd, specifically those immersed in the relevant expertise. By seeking input on the extent of expertise and identifying the individuals recognized as experts by their peers, we leverage a more informed and comprehensive approach. Luckily, our client agreed to this approach, as not a single expert identified by the wisdom of the crowd was on the list identified by headquarters.

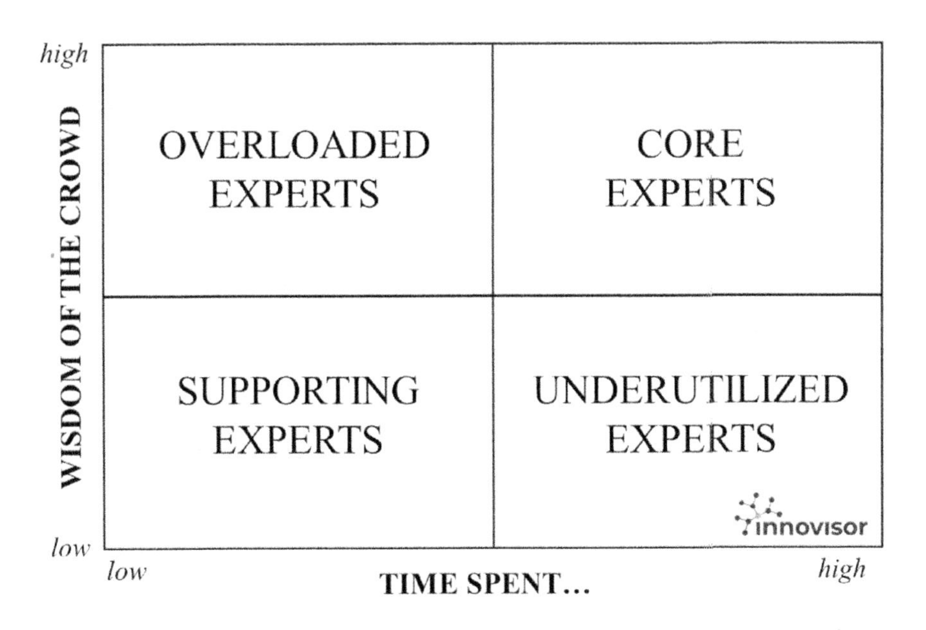

Figure 6: The different roles you have in communities based on their time spent on a topic and the awareness of others that you have this expertise.

In such a scenario, one can either go with the flow of the organization or try to work against it. Our client decided to go with the flow. They established connections with previously undiscovered experts, ensuring these individuals underwent comprehensive and current training in their respective domains. Activities were then organized and centered around their areas of expertise, creating a collaborative environment. To enhance visibility within the organization, strategies such as internal TED-like Tech talks were implemented, fostering widespread learning and knowledge dissemination.

Five years later the Cross-Organizational Centers of Expertise built on the input from the wisdom of the crowd are still perceived as breakthrough organizational design thinking in the industry.

Final Remarks

Cross-organizational connectivity does not happen by itself. As a leader, it is your responsibility to figure out appropriate connections, determining who should be connected, for what purpose, when, and why. Once these connections are identified, it becomes crucial to assign meaningful collaborative tasks. This not only allows individuals to get to know each other's competencies, but also fosters a sense of mutual understanding and sympathy over time.

Building connectivity between people across an organization is not a swift solution, but it is a magical recipe for long-term success.

Lessons Learned & Takeaways:

Chapter 6 uncovers that saving silos is the recipe to improve innovation and agility. Silos, often misunderstood, harbor strength. It is all about preserving their virtues, strategically connecting them for enhanced innovation. The three key insights unravel the power within, guiding leaders to navigate the complexity of organizational change and emerge as agile “speed boats.”

1. **See Silos as a Strength**

   Embrace silos for their positive attributes—closeness, trust, and a sense of belonging. Recognize them as a unique advantage that contributes to organizational efficiency and social capital.

2. **Transform Silos Into "Speedboats"**

   Utilize silos strategically, preserving their benefits while connecting them for increased agility and innovation. Shift from the notion of breaking down silos to leveraging them as a foundation for organizational speed and adaptability.

3. **Strategic connectivity for innovation**

   Foster cross-silo connectivity with a focused approach, connecting the right individuals for engagement, alignment, and innovation. Prioritize a small percentage of employees to bridge silos, promoting collaboration and breakthrough thinking for long-term organizational success.

Test Your Readiness – Are You Ready to Save The Silos and Become a Speedboat?

Is there an overall feeling inside the organizations that silos are a barrier and hurt innovation? Or do people recognize its value, but don't they know how to work with these silos? Answer the below questions and see if your organization is in the win, worry, or woe zone?

To what degree are silo viewed as an obstacle?	Minimal ☐	Moderate ☐	Significant ☐
To what extent is innovation currently hindered by siloed structures	Minimal ☐	Moderate ☐	Significant ☐
Is there a plan in place to strategically connect silos for agility?	Yes ☐	Partly ☐	No ☐
How open are people to cross-silo collaboration and knowledge sharing?	Very ☐	Moderate ☐	Limited ☐
	Win zone	Worry zone	Woe zone

References & Further Reading to Chapter 6

- Hansgaard, J. (2018) Stop Breaking Down the Silos. Save Them!, available on: https://www.linkedin.com/pulse/stop-breaking-down-silos-save-them-jeppe-vilstrup-hansgaard/

- Hansgaard, J. (2021) The Unharvested Potential of Organizational Bridges, available on: https://www.linkedin.com/pulse/unharvested-potential-organizational-bridges-jeppe-vilstrup-hansgaard/

- Hansgaard, J. (2023) Being International About 'WHO' is Key to Human-to-Human Connectivity, available on: https://www.linkedin.com/pulse/being-intentional-who-key-human-to-human-connectivity-hansgaard/

- Hansgaard, J. (2023) Massive Potential in Expertise Networks and Shadow Organizations, available on: https://www.linkedin.com/pulse/massive-potential-expertise-networks-shadow-jeppe-vilstrup-hansgaard/

- Hansgaard, J. (2023) Restructuring Does Not Remove Silos! People Do!, available on: https://www.linkedin.com/pulse/restructuring-does-remove-silos-people-do-jeppe-vilstrup-hansgaard/

- Hansgaard, J. (2023) Strong Hierarchies + Network Centricity = Amazing Results?, available on: https://www.linkedin.com/pulse/strong-hierarchies-network-centricity-amazing-results-hansgaard/

- Innovisor (2023) How LifeScienceCo Improved Its Connectivity, available on: https://www.innovisor.com/2023/01/26/how-lifescienceco-improved-its-connectivity-while-the-world-fell-apart/

CHAPTER SEVEN DIVERSITY, EQUITY, & INCLUSION – *LESS SUBJECTIVITY, MORE EVIDENCE*

"When people know they might have to explain their decisions, they are less likely to act on bias."

– Innovisor

Chapter 7: Diversity, Equity, & Inclusion – Less Subjectivity, More Evidence

"Hmm… We know that!"

I just boarded a plane from Frankfurt, Germany to Hanoi, Vietnam and had grabbed the newest edition of the local newspaper Frankfurter Allgemeine to entertain myself on the long flight. I flipped through the pages until my eyes stumbled on a small notice about a Scottish research team that had established that an increased level of Oxytocin in your body made your more collaborative.

Oxytocin is the female caretaker hormone.

We did not use gender in our analysis of organizational network data Innovisor had collected over time. We could go back to add it as a means of analysis, but it would take some work!

Men and Women Connect the Same With Others

Long story short, I asked a Norwegian business analyst in Innovisor – her name was Ina – to do it, and then I almost forgot about it.

"There is no difference in how much men and women collaborate inside organizations."

It was not the answer I hoped to get.

I hoped we could confirm the story of the Scottish research team, and then use it to get into global media.

Both Men and Women Connect Predominantly with Their Own Gender

Little would I know that something much more marvelous was about to happen.

"Can you check, if there is a difference in WHO they collaborate with?"

My mind was looking for a potential comeback. We have built the Innovisor database, so we can slice and dice data very quickly to look for stories and insights. 5 minutes later Ina got back to me.

"Men are 40% more likely to collaborate with men, and women are 40% more likely to collaborate with women."

Both genders a much more likely to collaborate with a person of their own gender. This was applicable regardless of function, hierarchy, geography, or whatever bias we could think of.

The Story Went Viral

This story could reach global media, so we immediately pitched it to Wall Street Journal.

Less than two days later they called for an interview.

I was answering the phone, while driving my kids to track & field practice. I answered in short sentences.

Two days later the story was included in the Friday edition of Wall Street Journal (2012), and from there went viral to media all over the world.

Picture 2: Book cover of the international bestseller Lean In by Sheryl Sandberg

To our astonishment, Sheryl Sandberg, who was the Chief Operating Officer of Facebook at that time, read the article. Sandberg (2013) incorporated the Innovisor findings in her global business bestseller, Lean In, which was published six months later.

I am confident that you will recognize the book when see its cover.

Gender Ratios Hide Connectivity Issues

Sheryl Sandberg's book catapulted a worldwide movement towards measuring gender ratios, as Diversity, Equity, & Inclusion (DEI) professionals pushed for a more balanced representation and an easy way to measure and report progress.

This was also the case at an automotive company Innovisor worked with.

They had achieved a 29% representation of women in management of the organization and was widely considered a DEI success story.

The industry benchmark was at 15%, so they were doing twice as well.

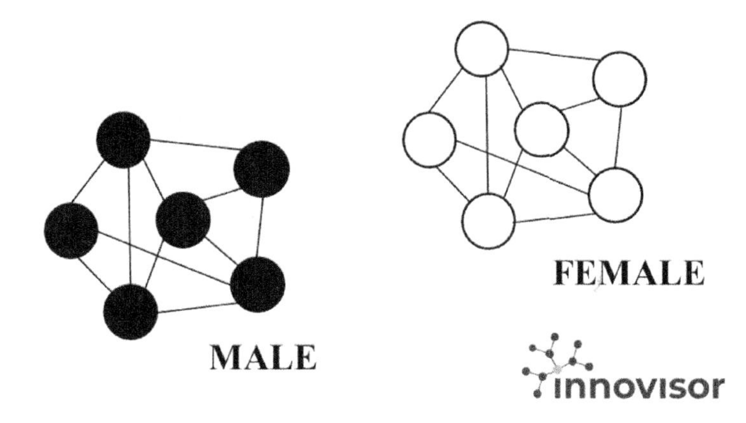

Illustration 4: Diversity is great; inclusion falls short.

However, there was a hidden issue.

The Innovisor assessment of connectivity revealed a problem. There were no connections at all between the female top-level managers and their male peers. 0% of the women on top-level management connected with men on top-level management. And vice versa.

Clearly, gender issues persisted beyond the glass ceiling. Ratios had not solved the issue.

So, how do you ensure connectivity between female and male leaders, if not with ratios?

Breaking the glass ceiling is not enough. You also need to tear down the walls! You need to fight unconscious biases in every single decision you face or action you take and create connectivity.

Fight Unconscious Biases in Every Decision

Have you restructured your organization, implemented a new operating model, or undertaken a large-scale organizational change program more than once? – Then you are likely making things worse on inclusion every single time you take a decision.

One engineering company we worked with struggled with the same issue. It was not until they shared how they spent the social time during leadership offsites that we found the solution. After full days in the meeting room, all the males would traditionally meet in the lounge bar to watch a soccer game, while the females either retracted to their rooms or went for a walk outside.

The solution was simple.

Find a new practice in the social time. Something that connects and includes all people. Something fun and playful.

It must be facilitated.

It cannot be left to chance.

Unconscious Biases Format and Categorize in Our Brain

Unconscious biases are present everywhere in our lives.

From the neighborhood we choose to live in, the close friends we have, to the people we date. Unconscious biases are formed throughout our life. We constantly gather millions of bits of information, and our brain processes that information in a certain way.

Categorizing and formatting it into familiar patterns. Something we can relate to and connect to.

Gender, ethnicity, disability, accents, sexuality, age, and so forth all influence our connections with others.

Regretfully, the consequence of our unconscious biases is exclusion.

Most know unconscious biases exist and that we should try to counter them!

Many companies – in the name of inclusion - offer training programs to make sure we know, how to fight it.

Evidence on Biases Is Absent in Decisions

But the knowledge is all wildly absent in our behaviors.

We need to integrate it into every single decision we make – daily, quarterly, or yearly – such as when we set-up new project teams, delegate roles and responsibilities or just decide, who is picking up coffee from the coffee machine and all the way to organization restructurings, implementation of new operating models, or large-scale change.

If we ignore our unconscious biases here, then we make things worse.

Every time!

We fail to use the opportunities to strengthen inclusion through better connectivity. To make sure people get to know each other, gain sympathy for each other, and have fun together.

And then our unconscious biases take over.

Things get worse.

More of the same.

Exclusion!

Current DEI Practices Do Not Help Inclusion Efforts!

Since the book Lean In was published a decade ago, organizations have invested billions of dollars into breaking down gender biases. In training, in women in leadership programs, in communication and more.

Regretfully, the data collected by Innovisor indicates minimal improvement in these numbers.

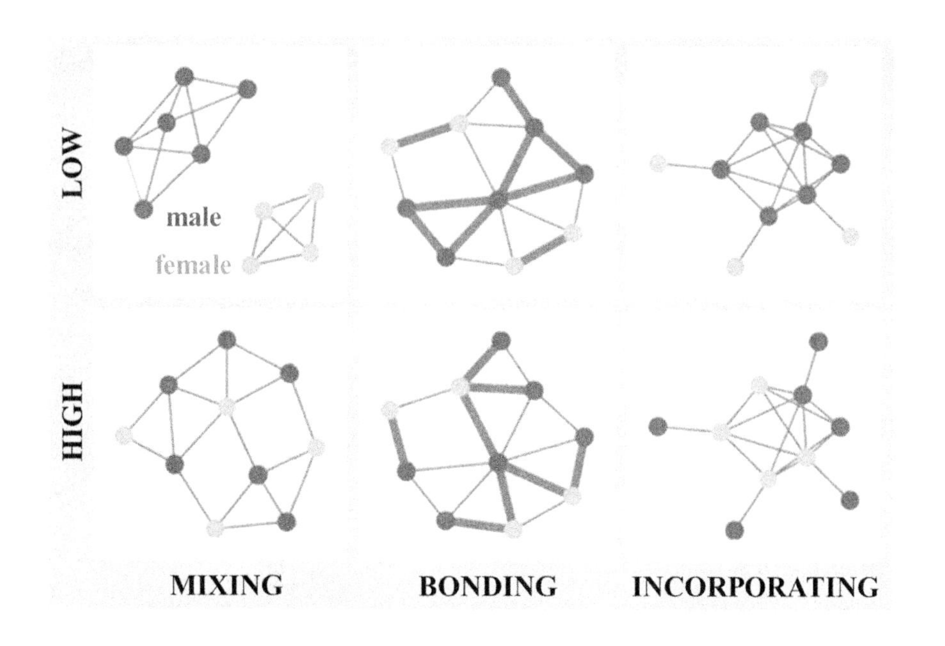

Network visual 4: Gender Connectivity (Source: Vedres & Vasarhelyi, 2022)

The Innovisor numbers in 2023 are:

Men are 30% more likely to collaborate with men. Women are 30% more likely to collaborate with women. Only slight improvement from a decade ago.

If you look in the illustration, it is evident that these two genders are still "low mixing" to "low bonding," whereas I think we can agree that we should aim for "high mixing" to "high bonding." It creates better performance and better wellbeing.

It Is Time for Change

DEI has become an industry and a profession, and it is not working. What you learn in a training session is forgotten shortly after, if not applied in practice.

To change for the better requires a much more intentional and fact-based approach. Below are the steps I recommend, which you can implement after mapping connectivity in your organization and incorporating gender attributes, and potentially other DEI attributes.

- Commit visibly to making a real difference. Set your target. Not just one that looks good on paper. Use the Gender Connectivity illustration from before.
- Communicate your target openly!
- Collect and share the evidence on your biases. Remember people are less likely to act biased when they must justify their actions.
- Connect people across divides intentionally.
- Listen to and act on feedback from tribes, groups, and cliques in your organization.
- Treat inclusion as an ongoing change.

Improved Inclusion Leads to Better Performance

It is no longer a novel claim that inclusion is a key impact variable for connectivity and wellbeing, which in turn drives better performance.

Isaac & McBurnie (2015) report in their book Close the Interaction Gap that 79% of a team's potential is lost because people fail to tap into the knowledge and expertise of their colleagues. Not least as they do not connect across the DEI barriers created by unconscious biases.

Leading companies in engineering, manufacturing and energy industries harvest the performance gains to be made through fighting unconscious biases and creating connectivity. Failing to improve connectivity across gender, age, ethnicity, accents, and sexuality results is a missed opportunity to outperform your competition.

What are you waiting for?

Final Remarks

We can only succeed if fighting unconscious biases becomes a movement. If it becomes unacceptable to not be inclusive. If it becomes a habit!

On behalf of my daughters, I will thank you for creating real change in the workplace on this front.

Finally, in the words of Mark Twain, remember this: "Whenever you find yourself on the side of the majority, it is time to pause and reflect."

Lessons Learned & Takeaways:

Chapter 7 displays surprising insights about collaboration patterns between diversity, equity, and inclusion barriers, such as genders. These findings challenge conventional Diversity, Equity, & Inclusion practices, emphasizing the need for intentional efforts to address unconscious biases and foster genuine connectivity for improved organizational performance. The three lessons learned, and key takeaways are:

1. **Gender Shapes Collaboration**

   Men and women are 40% more likely to collaborate with their own gender, transcending functions, hierarchy, and geography. The Innovisor study challenges assumptions, revealing the impact of oxytocin in collaboration and prompting a global media frenzy, even catching the attention of Facebook's Sheryl Sandberg.

2. **Connectivity Trumps Ratios**

   Beyond achieving numerical diversity, Innovisor uncovers a hidden issue in a seemingly successful Diversity, Equity, & Inclusion case. A company with 29% women in management lacked connectivity between genders, emphasizing that breaking the glass ceiling isn't enough; it requires dismantling the walls and addressing unconscious biases.

3. **Fight Biases in Decisions**

   Unconscious biases persist in organizational decisions, from project teams to social time during leadership offsites. The chapter advocates for a fundamental change in approach, urging companies to integrate awareness of biases into daily decisions. Ignoring biases hinders inclusion and perpetuates the cycle of exclusion.

Test Your Readiness – Are You Ready to Take Diversity, Equity, & Inclusion to the Next Level?

Embarking on the journey to advance Diversity, Equity, & Inclusion within your organization requires a nuanced understanding of the insights shared in this chapter. Answer the following questions and assess your readiness to propel Diversity, Equity, & Inclusion to the next level. Are you in the win, worry, or woe zone?

Does your organization recognize the importance of connectivity beyond achieving gender ratios?	**Fully recognize** ☐	**Partially recognize** ☐	**Not recognize** ☐
Is there a commitment to integrate awareness of unconscious biases into daily decision-making processes?	**Fully committed** ☐	**Partially committed** ☐	**Not committed** ☐
Are you or your organization aware that (gender) ratios may not necessarily indicate true inclusion?	**Very aware** ☐	**Somewhat aware** ☐	**Not aware** ☐
To what extent do you think traditional Diversity, Equity, & Inclusion training programs have effectively translated into behavioral changes in organizational decisions	**Ineffective** ☐	**Somewhat effective** ☐	**Highly effective** ☐
How willing is your organization to treat inclusion efforts as an ongoing, adaptive change rather than a one-time initiative?	**Very willing** ☐	**Somewhat willing** ☐	**Not willing** ☐
	Win zone	**Worry zone**	**Woe zone**

References & Further Reading to Chapter 7

- Isaac, M. & McBurnie, A. (2015) *Close the Interaction Gap: Discover, Harness, and Accelerate the Collaborative Potential of your Leaders, Teams, and Organization*, Bridge Publishing, ISBN: 978-0986295607

- Sandberg, S. (2013) *Lean In: Women, Work, and the Will to Lead*, Knopf, IBN: 978-0385349949

- Vedres, B. & Vasarhelyi (2022) Inclusion Unlocks the Creative Potential of Gender Diversity in Teams, in: *Computer Science*, available on: https://arxiv.org/abs/2204.08505

- Wall Street Journal (2012) At Work, in: *Wall Street Journal*, available on: https://www.wsj.com/articles/SB10001424052702303506404577448652549105934

CHAPTER EIGHT HYBRID WORK – *NOT A ONE-SIZE-FITS-ALL SOLUTION*

"When the map is not reflecting the terrain,

follow the terrain."

– Military Principle

Chapter 8: Hybrid Work – Not a One-Size-Fits-All Solution

March 10, 2020, about 5:45 A.M. I read a text message from my colleague.

"We will be working on 'Teams' from now on."

The pandemic had arrived in Denmark. The night before the Danish Prime Minister Mette Frederiksen had in a – what will be known as a historic press conference – announced that Denmark closed all public institutions and encouraged companies to do the same. Infection numbers were on the rise.

"Teams?"

I recalled having seen that logo somewhere on my laptop but had never used it.

"Denmark closed… what about my kids?"

I was in Moldova facilitating workshops, conducting stakeholder interviews as a follow-up of a major analysis, and to lead change leadership training for the UN agencies in the country.

As always, I would go for my morning run to clear my mind and think through what to do.

This morning the weather was beautiful, with the sun rising on the horizon. There was frost in the air. I enjoyed the stabilizing impact of the running on my concerned mood.

Running always helps me.

Picture 3: From the Morning run on March 10, 2020, in Chisinau, Moldova (Source: Jeppe Vilstrup Hansgaard)

During the run I made three decisions:

- People must always come first. Make sure everybody in Innovisor is in the know all the time. Also, for the tough decisions.
- Let's do whatever we can to help our clients get through this unprecedented challenge with the capabilities we have. Reconfigure the Innovisor tools, so we can tell where their leadership will have the biggest impact in the coming weeks and months. Do this for FREE.
- Share the learning from here with the Innovisor community, so everybody benefits.

Little would I know that those decisions became the foundation for how we in Innovisor still work four years later.

The pandemic catalyzed a new way of working that none of us could have imagined.

The Dramatic Impact of Pandemic on Connectivity

The impact of the pandemic was quickly visible in the organizational network data we collect in Innovisor.

- We saw how new hires in the period from March to September 2020 struggled to get integrated into organizations. Time-to-Integration doubled. Especially young professionals starting in the first job and senior experts expected to deliver from day one suffered. This lack of integration was still visible for the group two years later and to a lesser extent today.

- We saw people dropping out of the informal networks in unprecedented numbers. Whereas pre-pandemic was about 5% that nobody reached to for help and advice or the social chit chat inside organizations, the number grew to 30% before the end of the summer 2020. In December 2023, at the time of writing, the number is still around 24%.
- We saw overall fragmentation of collaboration networks. Especially cross-connectivity in organizations suffered, as people stayed in contact with their strong connections inside their own teams, but not with those individuals from other teams that they before would have made in the corridor or in the canteen.

Quickly new working models materialized. At first 100% remote work models gained popularity – especially with technology companies.

Since, hybrid work became what most organizations settled for and now struggle with. The hybrid work models implemented have regretfully accelerated the fragmentation inside organizations.

The Biggest Change to Work in My Lifetime

The arrival of hybrid work has been the biggest change to how work gets done in organizations in my lifetime.

Still, I did not feel like including a chapter on hybrid work in this book around broken connectivity. It was a topic so many people had written emotionally about, so what could I add to the discussion? The answer was data! Just like in those early days of the pandemic.

Leaders Resist Change

When I entered the corporate world many, many years ago the mention of hybrid work models would have resulted in eyes rolling and silent giggling.

"Presenteeism" was the name of the game, and us young employees often stuck around not only until the workday was over – but until our direct leader was leaving the office. Who, again, stayed until their leader left the office.

The attitude towards leaving the office at the end of the workday before your leader has softened over the years. However, when the pandemic arrived in 2020, presence was still valued by leaders when evaluating individual performance.

Since, we have had the greatest work experiment ever…driven by a pandemic.

Not by the sudden desire from leaders ready to change the work model that made them surface at the top of the organizational hierarchy.

Hence, many leaders resist the change brought about through these new hybrid work models.

They want their people back in the office five days per week.

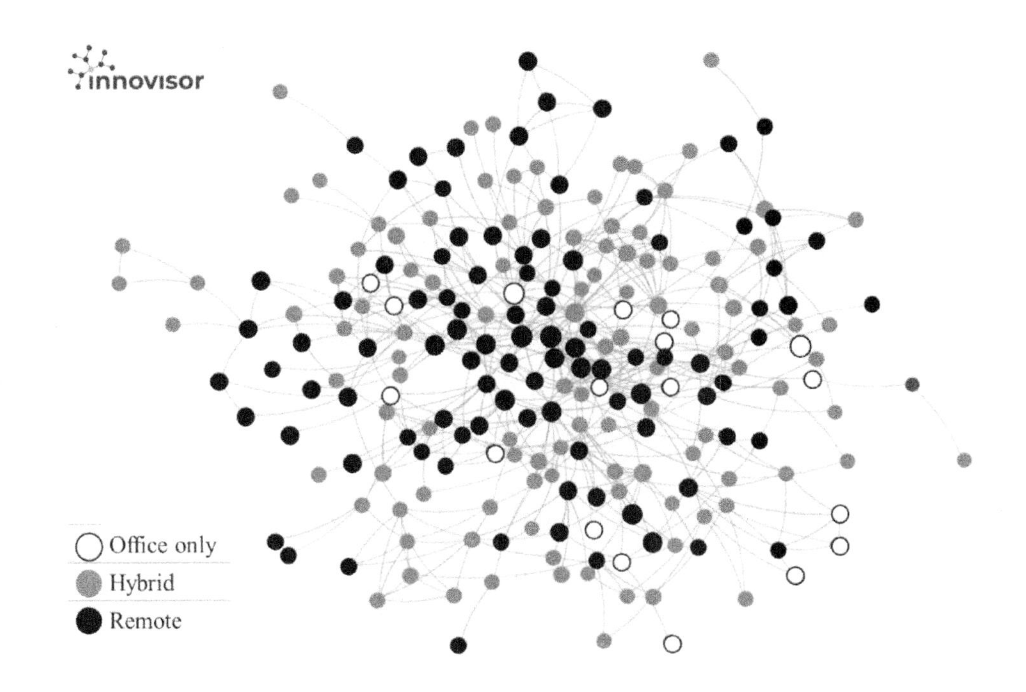

Network visual 5: Hybrid Working and Team Connectivity

I must admit this is hard for me to understand.

Work performance has never been about the days in the office. It has always been about what happens when you are together. How intentional you are.

The Hybrid Work Principles of Innovisor

In Innovisor, we have defined and agreed principles for what we want to meet for (Hansgaard, 2021). Those principles are all about the value-add of being and working together.

We meet for:

1. **Kickstarting New Projects and Initiatives:** where we align roles and responsibilities, agree on timelines, milestones, success criteria, etc.
2. **Complex Problem Solving:** we benefit from being able to work together in the same room on a problem. From walking back and forth between a white board or a flip chart. To allow for small breaks and then meet again.
3. **Onboarding of New Employees:** there is no substitute for meeting face-to-face when you have new joiners. We invest significantly in making sure they feel welcome and that they have one-on-ones with everybody they need to work closely with.

4. **Fun and Teambuilding:** importantly, this must be as part of the workday. Quizzes, games, jokes… you got it. And again, this works best, when you meet face to face.

For everything else, people decide for themselves. Some prefer to go to the office every day, because they have too much noise in their homes. Others – like me – prefer the solitude of their home. In my case, especially when I prepare for seminars, lectures or write articles.

Leaders Love Data

Since the pandemic started, Innovisor has studied the hybrid work patterns inside organizations and listened to the many different opinions and seen the different approaches to hybrid work.

Leadership has struggled to elevate performance, and employees have found it challenging to fully embrace the hybrid work.

The Innovisor Hybrid Work Study

In May 2023, Innovisor launched a hybrid work study with 2,000+ employees from four companies across Europe.

The question we wanted to answer was: Is there one hybrid work model supporting high performance?

From our past studies, we knew that great connectivity in organizational networks leads to high performance, agility of knowledge flows, better innovation, improved employee retention, and faster change adaptation. Our emphasis in this study was really about how you can keep connectivity intact, while you work hybrid.

Here are the two take-aways from studying.

Take-Away #1: One Best Hybrid Work Model Does Not Exist

There is no best one-size-fits-it-a high-performing hybrid work model. All organizations and functions are unique, and the diversity of business models results in significant disparities when it comes to hybrid work.

Company Alpha: The Innovisor Hybrid Work Study revealed that more than 80% of employees at Company Alpha spend fewer than two days per week in the office. Notably, their connectivity to collaboration and social networks peaked when they spent one day per week in the office.

Company Bravo: In stark contrast, more than 50% of employees at Company Bravo expressed reached the best connectivity to collaboration and social network, when they spent three or more days in the office per week.

Company Charlie & Company Delta: Similar differences were seen in Company Charlie and Company Delta.

For these companies one uniform hybrid work model for high performance did not exist. We could even see that various models were needed to achieve high connectivity inside the companies. E.g. when comparing the HR function with the Sales function.

So, can organizations apply the same hybrid work model to optimize performance?

Like, when some organizations impose a three days per week in the office model.

It is impossible! Doing that is poor leadership. Some functions in organizations will benefit from three days in the office. Others from one day in the office and again others from five days in the office. It is widely dependent on the work that needs to be done, the culture and especially how it is facilitated.

If you get to the office, but the people you are supposed to engage with are not there, and you as consequence sit the entire day in virtual meeting, then the negative impact on performance is evident. When people go to the office, it should be with an intent to meet specific people for a purpose.

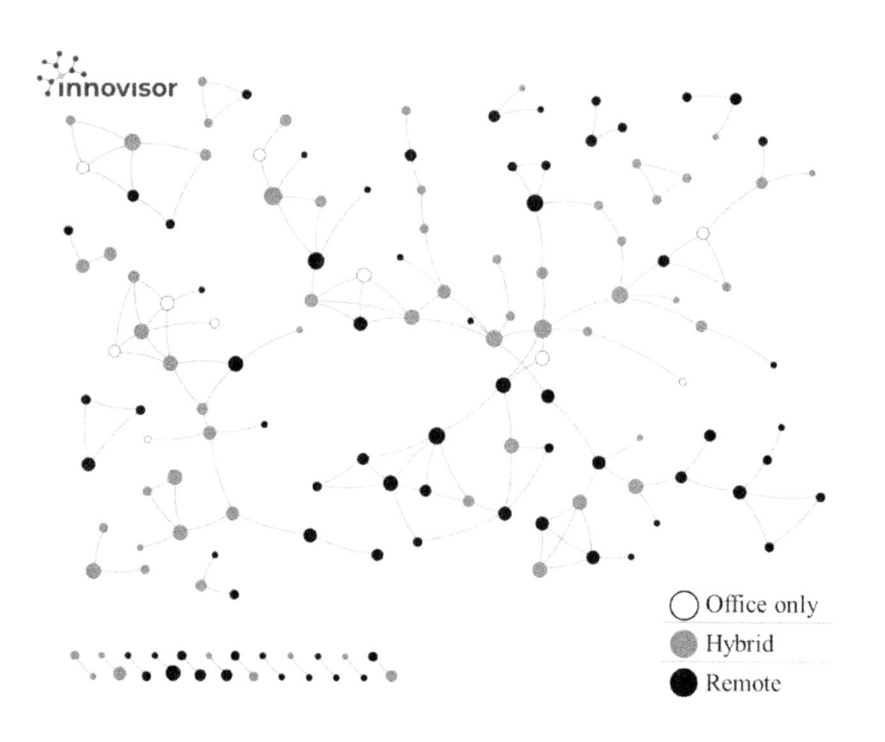

Network visual 6: The connectivity of company Delta

Take-Away #2: Understand Trade-Offs for High-Performance

Defining this requires a deep understanding of the trade-offs that the hybrid work model is built upon. Great leaders know they need to understand the trade-offs in their hybrid work models, and that they to need engage their people in the tailoring of the design.

Imposing a hybrid work model top-down is a recipe for disaster.

In our study, we observed how a global organization hastily implemented a three-day office-two-day remote hybrid work system without thoughtful consideration. This rushed decision ultimately resulted in a quick drop in employee retention and Engagement. Primarily because the impractical hybrid work model failed to foster intentional connections among employees.

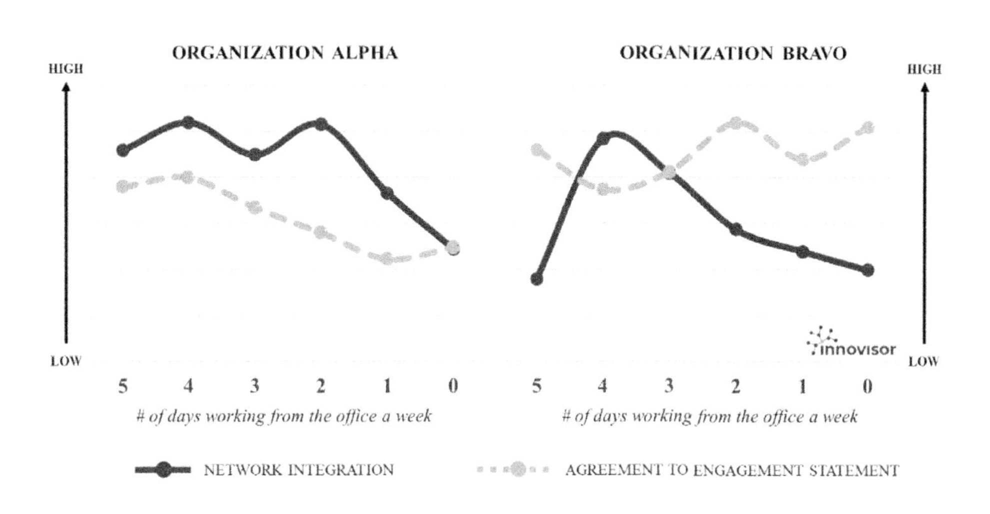

Illustration 5: There is no one-size-fits-all solution to hybrid work

While a tailored hybrid work solution designed together with the employees is a promising start. Don't think you are done!

Change is constant, both internally and externally. Successful leadership of hybrid work proactively embraces ongoing change. As a leader you must continuously listen to your workforce and identify how your business evolves, so you can recalibrate your hybrid work model to meet evolving needs and ensure high-performance. I recommend you revisit your hybrid work models at least once per year. You might as well integrate into your annual wheel, as something you consider doing the strategy process together with your people (Innovisor, 2023).

Final Remarks

The key question you must ask yourself is does our current hybrid work model achieve is what we want it to achieve. To answer this question, you must gather the data and engage your people. Without their involvement you can never make it a success.

After all, done by the people and done with the people always beats done to the people!

Lessons Learned & Takeaways:

Chapter 8 discusses a people-first approach for hybrid work, and the need to explore a diversity of hybrid work models. The three lessons learned and key takeaways are:

1. **Prioritize People**

   When you place people at the forefront in your hybrid work decision, you must adopt transparent communication. This ensures that everyone, even during tough decisions, remains well-informed so that you can foster a culture of trust and unity within the organization.

2. **No One-Size-Fits-All**

   Reject a one-size-fits-all approach by recognizing the organizational complexities. You must tailor your hybrid work arrangements based on unique functions and contexts that are part of the norm, acknowledging the varied needs and nuances within the workforce.

3. **Hybrid Work is Dynamic**

   Ensure you view hybrid work as a dynamic, ever-evolving initiative. You must emphasize the importance of continual adaptation. This requires a proactive stance — regularly listening to the workforce, recalibrating models, and involving employees in the iterative process for sustained high performance.

Test Your Readiness – Are You Ready to Understand Hybrid Work Dilemmas?

Answer the next questions on communication, adaptability, leadership, and more to assess your organization's readiness to navigate the dynamic landscape of hybrid work. Are you in the win, worry, or woe zone?

Have your organization previously experienced hybrid work arrangements?	**Yes** ☐	**Somewhat** ☐	**No** ☐
How aligned do you think your current leadership is with embracing hybrid work?	**Fully aligned** ☐	**Partially aligned** ☐	**Not aligned** ☐
How intentional do you believe your organization must be in visiting the office?	**Very intentional** ☐	**Moderately intentional** ☐	**Not intentional** ☐
How well does your leaders understand the trade-offs involved in hybrid work models?	**Very well** ☐	**Somewhat well** ☐	**Not well** ☐
How committed is your organization in ongoing changed to the hybrid work model	**Very committed** ☐	**Somewhat committed** ☐	**Not committed** ☐
	Win zone	**Worry zone**	**Woe zone**

References & Further Reading to Chapter 8

- Hansgaard, J.V. (2022) Hybrid Work is Real – How we do it in Innovisor, available on: https://www.linkedin.com/pulse/hybrid-work-real-how-we-do-innovisor-jeppe-vilstrup-hansgaard/

- Innovisor (2023) The Right Thing to Do in a Hybrid Work Environment, available on: https://www.innovisor.com/2023/07/19/the-right-thing-to-do-in-a-hybrid-work-environment/

CHAPTER NINE MERGERS & ACQUISITIONS – *PROTECT THE INVESTMENT, PEOPLE OVER PROCESSES & SYSTEMS*

"Value creation only happens after the acquisition when people from both organizations collaborate."

– Haspeslagh & Jemison

Chapter 9: Mergers & Acquisitions – *Protect the Investment, People Over Processes & Systems*

Five Years of Persistence to Create Change

I chit-chat with all the people I meet throughout the day. I believe every encounter for me is an opportunity to spark a little joy in the life of someone else. Mostly I get positive feedback.

Though admitted sometimes it takes longer than expected. Like when I moved to where I live now and smiled and waved good morning to those, I met during my morning run. At first, they looked angry, then they started to cross the street to avoid me, but nine years later they finally smiled back and said good morning.

I believe it took me five years of persistence to create the change.

The disconnect caused by mergers & acquisitions (M&A) integration mostly takes more than five years to solve. People have much more feelings involved than when they meet their new neighbor out for his morning run.

How A Casual Meeting in the Kindergarten Helped

The CEO personally selected me and four others to spearhead the integration with the other company. Although both companies now shared a physical location, they were situated as far apart as possible within the building.

Except for our little five-person integration team. We were sent 'behind enemy lines' tasked with 'fixing' the integration by the CEO.

I tried my usual approach. A smile and a loud good morning.

No response. Just silence. It felt odd.

I found a desk. Picked up my laptop. Started working. I could always do my e-mails.

Everybody stared at me. They whispered to each other.

At lunchtime they got up and left. They didn't include me.

The next day, I had caught on, so I followed them. There was no space for me at any of their tables.

Three months in I was still not getting any response to my good mornings or my smiles, and I was still eating lunch by myself.

Probably one of the hardest times of my work life. I promised myself I would NEVER get personally involved in an M&A integration project again.

But then it happened… one of the assistants from "the other" company noticed me at an event in the kindergarten of my son, where her daughter also went. I was my normal self, and we started to talk. The setting was different and that made it possible. I guess it was hard for her not to say hi when I smiled.

At least that was the turning point where the divide between me and the other company abruptly softened, and the barriers between the two companies got less stiff.

Effects Are Visible 10 Years Later

"What is that? We cannot explain it."

When I hear the Innovisor Center of Excellence say this when they diagnose the informal networks of our clients, I have learned always to consider the aftermaths of a merger first.

The first time I experienced this, I called the Group CFO to discuss. We talked for 20 minutes. I could not explain a very tightly knitted cluster of 30 people spread across six locations, and only connected to all others through one person.

I shared names, responsibilities, and all other information I had access to. 20 minutes is a long time, when you have no clue what is going on. I am sure the Group CFO was not feeling comfortable with this.

"It is the acquisition we did four years ago," the Group CFO suddenly stuttered. He had seen the connection in all what I shared.

For the first time they had an explanation why they had not realized the value of the acquisition they had made.

The Group CFO had not noticed the disconnect, as he was only connected to the affiliate leadership team. They had assured him that the integration was running according to plan.

In similar ways, we have seen through our work in Innovisor:

- Financial Institutions are still struggling with integration more than ten years after they had been merged. Almost dividing into groups determined by the colors of their former company logos. Are you on the blue team or the red team? Secretly nodding to each other, when passing each other on the stairs – or even worse keeping company traditions and get-together of the old company alive, but not inviting anyone from 'the other team'.
- Municipalities that over ten years after being merged – dictated by a governmental reform – still did not connect across the old borders. Yes, they were sitting in the same building – but they still prioritized legacy colleagues, when they went for lunch or needed help and advice.

Case: The Merger That Went All Wrong

Two US based trading companies of equal size were merged into one, and immediately after the final sign off moved into a new, shared building for its 600 employees. It was indeed the intention of the leadership and owners to make sure this was a merger of true equals, with none of the employees having the privilege of a legacy. Investments were made into a new company name, logo, visual identity, and a new president from the outside was brought in.

Now, synergies were to be harvested through collaboration, innovation, and development.

Two years later, something did not "smell right" to the owners. Obvious synergies had not been harvested, and Innovisor was brought in to assess connectivity.

Connectivity was still low. The catalysts in the informal networks – the 3% that shaped the commitment – had never been activated and engaged in the post-merger integration process and disliked it as a result.

Only 50% of them felt informed about the process, less than 25% agreed with the objectives formulated two years earlier, and 0% saw the leaders as visible role models.

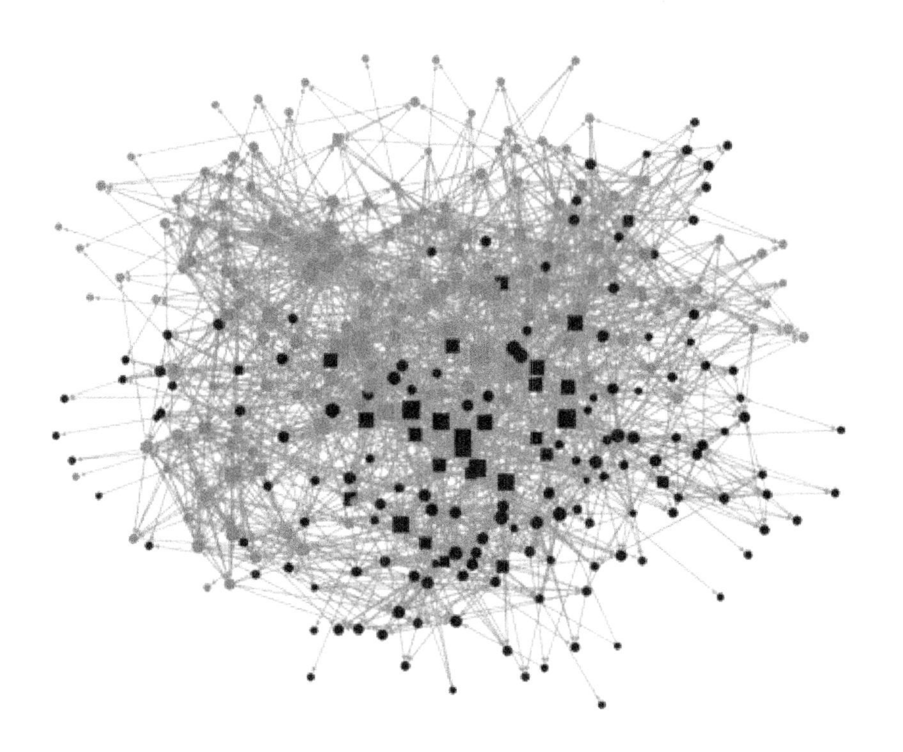

Network visual 7: The two legacy companies are shown by their colors.

The 3%, aka "the catalysts," play a pivotal role for any merger to succeed, and in this case, they had been ignored.

Resistance was growing quickly.

Similarly, no people integration efforts had been made outside the three top layers of leadership. People did not know who to reach out to from the other company if they wanted to solve a problem or discuss a new idea. Thus, it became easier just to work with your legacy colleagues and ignore the opportunities offered by the new colleagues.

I asked myself, could this merger still be saved?

70-90% Of Mergers Go Wrong

It is not surprising that mergers fail. Research consistently reports that 70-90% of mergers fail to deliver on their intentions (Aon Hewitt, 2011). It is more surprising that organizations still reach out to the same handbook, when everybody knows it brings such mediocre results.

Mergers can vary greatly and therefore the causes of failure may be completely different from case to case. However, research reveals that challenges around people and culture are pre-dominantly mentioned as the main cause of failed integration. That shouldn't come as a surprise, as people and culture are essential to the success of every organizational initiative. When organizations deal with mergers, people and culture always seem to land at the bottom of the priority lists, whereas more tangible tasks receive the attention.

What You Should Do Instead

The Innovisor four-step approach for improving connectivity in an M&A is:

- Step 1 - Assess Informal Connectivity.
- Step 2 – Identify, Activate, and Engage Informal Catalysts.
- Step 3 - Understand Emotions and Commitment.
- Step 4 – Track Consistently.

Let me walk you through the steps.

Step 1 - Assess Informal Connectivity

The first step is to assess the real connectivity inside and across the organizations. Depending on timing you look for different things (more on that a bit later.)

Are there any evolving connections between the two companies that can be utilized? Are the two companies lead very differently, e.g. one is hierarchical and the other one is flat? – Is connectivity within limited, extensive, or at the same level? Are there invisible silos? – and who are the key people to retain and activate?

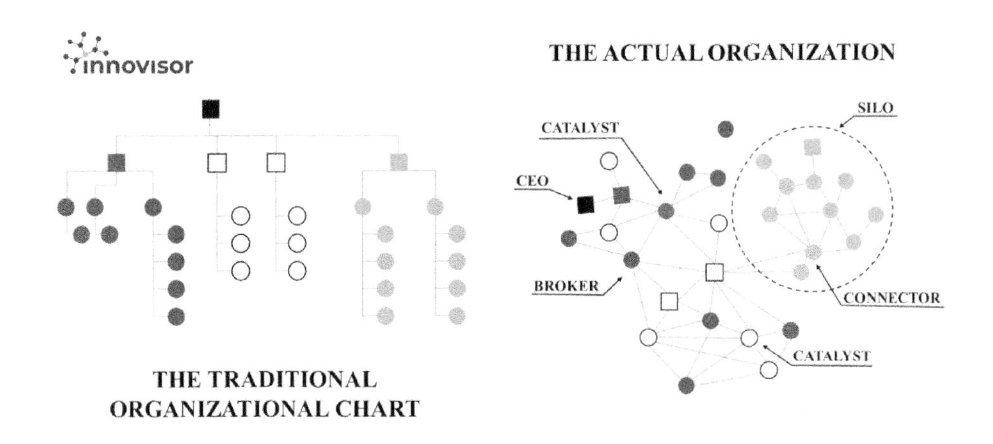

Illustration 6: The Power of Network Analysis

Step 2 – Identify, Activate, and Engage Informal Catalysts

When you have assessed the connectivity, you must identify the informal catalysts. The catalysts are pivotal for one specific reason.

They must be retained.

In most cases, M&As result in employees leaving the company, voluntarily or not, and chances are that the catalysts are among these. Innovisor experience shows that although management believes they know who the key influencers are, they never do, and therein lies the danger. No one realizes their importance until they are gone. If the wrong person leaves, then leaving can become contagious.

In the past, Innovisor has measured an increase in the probability of other leaving of 500%, if one of these sympathetic, competent, and trustworthy individuals in the informal networks leave.

See an example in the illustration.

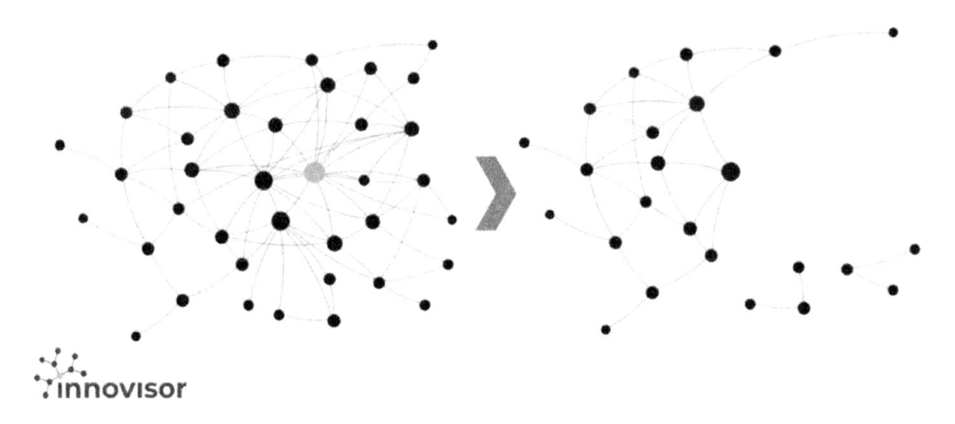

Network visual 8: Network simulation of what happens when an informal (shown in grey) leaves.

Step 3 - Understand Emotions and Commitment

During post-merger integration a lot of rumors can circulate amongst employees. Some of them will be made up, as people fill unknown spaces with their own stories. This can significantly reduce engagement and significantly impact performance.

Negativity is important to understand and address head on, rather than, what I unfortunately often see, avoided.

- Catalysts' emotions have ripple effects in the organization. It is tempting to simply get rid of the negative catalysts, but I would like to warn against this, as it can lead to contagious quitting. Instead, listen to and involve them. If you win their direct support, you accelerate winning the support of their peers. Their opinions are magnetic.

- Negativity in sub-groups, cliques, and tribes need to be. It needs to be encapsulated and receive separate attention, while all other post-merger activities move forward.

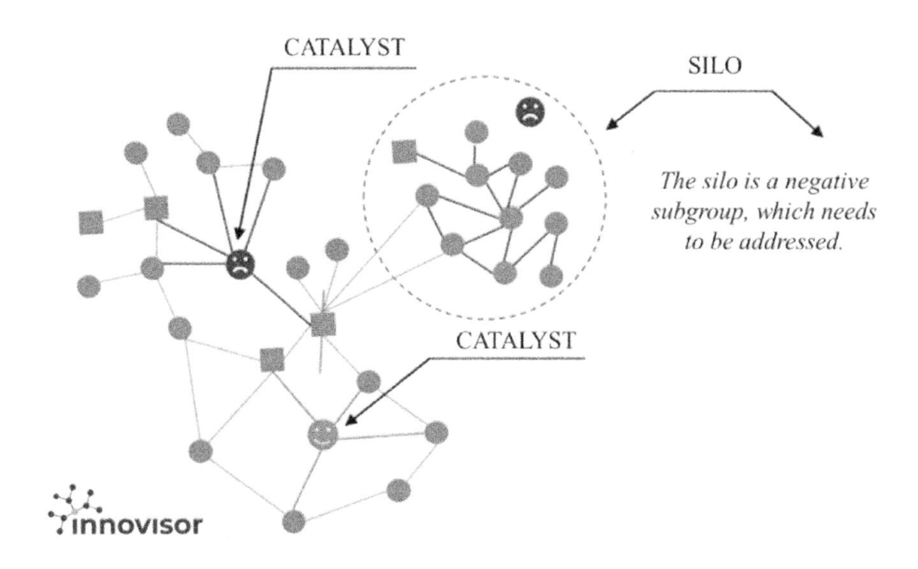

Illustration 7: Different key people inside the informal network with different levels of commitment and sentiment.

Having identified the key people to work with you need to activate and engage them in the post-merger activities.

How to do that is the topic of my first playbook Another Change Fiasco! Now What? (Hansgaard, 2023). If you are very interested, I recommend investing in this book.

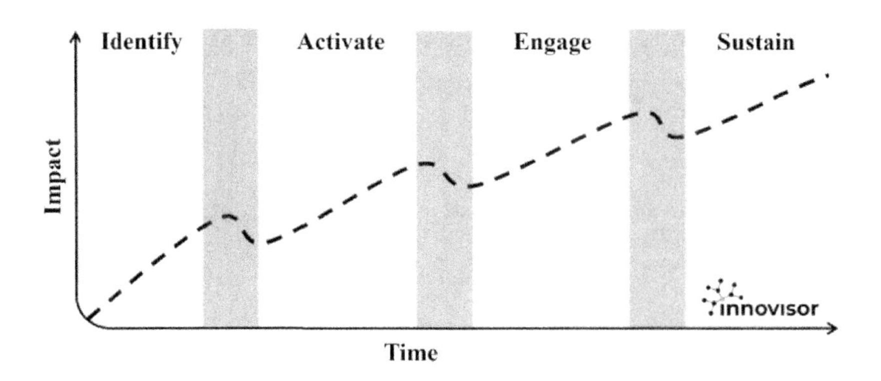

Figure 7: Innovisor Wave Model

Step 4 - Track consistently

Make sure you track the progress of the post-merger integration consistently. Tracking allows leaders to get valuable insight into the integration progress and calibrate the right actions at the right time, to ensure sustained success. Best practice is to track emotions and commitment around the merger every second month and the connectivity progress every twelve months.

Like this company did and realized that its integration was not working as expected.

The HR-director said: "Nobody told us why were supposed to work with them." So, no activities to connect people and culture were initiated.

After 12 months a comeback was still possible, but it required a dedicated project team and a leadership team that stayed on top of it. No doubt the integration team would have liked to realize this at an earlier stage.

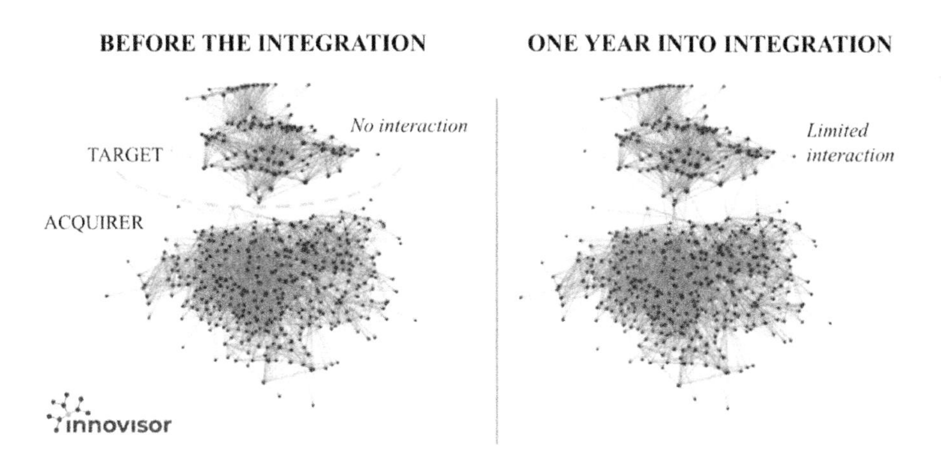

Network visual 9: The integration of two companies tracked overtime

When does it make sense to assess connectivity during a merger?

One question I often get is when it makes sense to assess the connectivity during a merger. Many leaders recognize the immense value associated with such assessments, as they effectively mitigate risks previously hidden.

My preference is to have access to the information on connectivity already before signing the final agreement. However, this is only possible if the acquired company has prepared itself by running an internal assessment first.

Alternatively, the only choice is to wait until post-merger. Here there are three options:

- **Immediate Assessment:** Conducting the evaluation right after the merger initiation ensures a proactive and accurate understanding from the outset.
- **Nine to Twelve Months After:** Opting for assessment within the nine to twelve months post-merger allows for a more calibrated and nuanced examination of connectivity dynamics.
- **Three-years Post-merger:** Delaying the evaluation until three years after the merger provides an opportunity for a comprehensive comeback, offering insights that may not be immediately apparent.

The value of each of these exercises is exceptionally high, with early assessments minimizing potential losses during the subsequent post-merger phase.

Case – Part Two: The Merger That Went All Wrong

Getting back to the case I mentioned earlier in this chapter.

Was it still possible to salvage the merger? Yes, it was. However, the efforts required to rescue it were considerably greater than if proactive measures around connectivity had been implemented from the beginning, identifying, activating, and engaging informal catalysts.

Now, this had to take place after 12 months. Some key people had left. A lot of people had probably considered it, and performance was at a lower level than expected.

They engaged people in focus groups and task forces, invited them to listening sessions. Leadership realized they needed to be vulnerable and acknowledge their mistakes. Apologizing to the people in the merged companies and promised a different path forward: Done **by** and done **with** the people. Not done **to** the people! This shift in approach played a pivotal role in assuaging trust concerns stemming from past experiences of empty leadership promises.

Based on feedback from these focus groups, leadership learned moving forward to prioritize face-to-face with employees over other means of communication. This gave leadership the opportunity to walk-the-walk (instead of just talk-the-talk) and role model what needed to take place and stayed on top of post-merger integration.

12 months later connectivity was reassessed, and improvement was clear.

They could return to their original objectives for the merger.

Final Remarks

In mergers, always remember you are dealing with humans with emotions. Prioritize that from the outset – not as the last point on the tick-off list. For some odd reason systems, structures, and processes always win in the integration phase…and that sets you up for failure.

Make the people your priority and show visible leadership.

Your key questions to answer are: Who needs to be retained? Who needs to be kept in the know? Who needs to be connected?

Lessons Learned & Takeaways:

Chapter 8 highlights the challenges of mergers and acquisitions, emphasis on prioritizing people over processes. The three lessons learned, and key takeaways are:

1. **Disconnect in M&A Takes Time to Resolve**

   Mergers & Acquisition challenges persist beyond five years. Emotional and cultural divides require extended efforts for resolution, emphasizing the enduring impact on organizational cohesion and performance.

2. **Neglect of People Integration Causes Failures**

   The 70-90% failure rate often stems from overlooking people and culture in mergers & acquisitions. Prioritizing tangible tasks over human aspects diminishes success, highlighting the necessity of placing people at the core of integration strategies.

3. **Four-Step Approach to M&A Success**

   Innovisor's strategy—Assess, Identify, Understand, Track—offers a holistic approach. By recognizing the importance of informal networks, emotions, and the consistent monitoring of these two areas enhance organizations' connectivity, mitigate risks, and achieve sustained success in post-merger scenarios.

Test Your Readiness – Are You Ready to Run a People-First Merger & Acquisition?

Navigating through mergers and acquisitions requires a strategic blend of foresight and adaptability. Success often hinges on the approach taken towards the most valuable asset - the people. Assess your organization's readiness for a people-first approach in the next mergers and acquisition initiative. Are you in the win, worry, or woe zone?

How regularly does the organization assess (informal) connectivity within and across teams during a merger?	**Regularly** ☐	**Sometimes** ☐	**Rarely** ☐
How effectively does the organization address and understand the emotions and commitment levels of employees during post-merger integration?	**Effectively** ☐	**Adequately** ☐	**Ineffectively** ☐
To what degree do leaders serve as visible role models during the post-merger phase?	**Consistently** ☐	**Sometimes** ☐	**Rarely** ☐
How well does the organization address negativity within sub-groups, cliques, and tribes during post-merger activities?	**Effectively** ☐	**Moderately** ☐	**Poorly** ☐
How consistently does the organization track emotions, commitment, and connectivity progress during the post-merger activities?	**Consistently** ☐	**Occassionally** ☐	**Infrequently** ☐
	Win zone	**Worry zone**	**Woe zone**

References & Further Reading to Chapter 9

- AON Hewitt (2011) Culture Integration in M&A: Survey Findings, available on: https://www.aon.com/attachments/thought-leadership/M_A_Survey.pdf

- Hansgaard, J. (2023) *Another Change Fiasco! Now What? Your Playbook to Activate the 3% You Need to Win Your Change*, Copenhagen: Innovisor Consulting, ISBN: 978-8797490303

CHAPTER TEN

A SUCCESS STORY – *CONNECTIVITY DRIVES SUPERIOR PERFORMANCE*

"Relationships are the fertile soil from which all advancement, all success, all achievement in real life grow."
– Ben Stein

Chapter 10: Success Story – Connectivity Drives Superior Performance

"WHAT?!?"

People normally praised him for his very analytical and calm attitude. His McKinsey-background probably helped here, but now he had difficulties in controlling his temper.

As a relatively new CEO of ManufacturingCo his primary focus had been on aggressive cost-cutting and shedding of underperforming businesses. He had personally been involved in how to sharply reduce development time for new products. Holding his temper was difficult, when he learned that they had probably lost several billion USD in the Christmas sales because the organization had ignored (or even blocked) the signals coming from the front lines about a fast-rising demand for a new product line.

Too many organizational layers filtered this business-critical information, and it had never reached the CEO and his team. The CEO swore that this would never happen again, while he oversaw ManufacturingCo.

What he did next earned him recognition as the best CEO in the world.

Hierarchy Blocks Information Up and Down

In December 2022, Meta (formerly known as Facebook) announced that they wanted to flatten their management chain. You might say with good reason, when you see a visualization of the many layers, they had between CEO Mark Zuckerberg and the people in the Meta organization.

11 layers in total.

Removing a few layers in the organizational chart would deliver a short-term cost reduction, but it would not change the ability of the company to achieve long-term success through market awareness, customer-centricity, innovation, and speed.

To achieve this, Meta was better recommended to pursue its original mission statement: "make the world more open and connected."

Just inside its own organization.

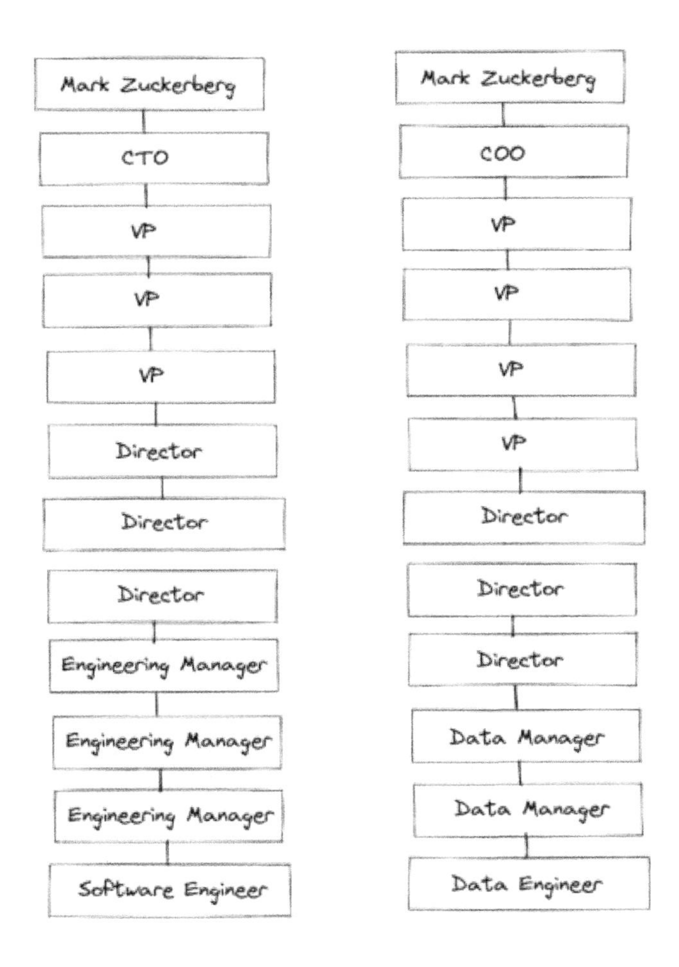

Illustration 8: Hierarchy Layers in Meta (Source: PragmaticEngineer.com)

Are 13 Levels the World Record for Organizational Hierarchies?

When I learned about the 11 layers of Meta, I was sure it had to be a world record… but then I asked the Innovisor Center of Excellence, what we had experienced in the past.

Our record witnessed at Innovisor was 12 layers in a 12,000-person technology organization!

I then asked on X (then known as Twitter), if anyone knew an organization with more than 12 layers and learned that Yahoo had 13 layers in 2004. THIRTEEN!!!

Is this then the world record? – or does anyone know of an organization with 14+ layers?

If you do, please send me a DM on LinkedIn or X. I promise to write a blog post about it and thank you publicly.

What Is the Implication of Hierarchies?

So why are traditional hierarchies bad? Well, they are not entirely bad.

They provide a lot of organizational clarity on who can decide on what. This benefit cannot be underestimated.

The downside, however, is that they create an over-focus on "inside-the-box" thinking and limited focus on "outside-the-box" or even "between-the-boxes" thinking. There is also another issue with hierarchies, which is specifically related to information sharing.

When critical information needs to be transferred upwards or downwards through steep hierarchies, it empowers the maximum number of people to hinder or slow down the bottom-up passage of business-critical information, before it reaches the people that need the information.

This is exactly what happened in ManufacturingCo! Somewhere between the frontlines, market forecasting, and product planning, someone actively decided to ignore or block the strong signals from the market.

How the CEO Role Modeled Network Centricity in a Hierarchical Organization

The CEO immediately requested a meeting with the regional sales leadership, the forecasting director, and the vice presidents of the biggest production facilities. Only to learn that they could have sold ten times as much as they did, if only the forecasting had been more accurate.

The new CEO was visibly fuming. His tall stature looked very tense. Close to explosion.

How could they miss the target by so much? He looked towards the forecasting director. This needed to change immediately. His own initial thought was “we need a new IT-system, so we can predict with greater accuracy.” SAP had always been his go-to solution, and he had good connections to the south German company.

“It is a people issue!”

To his surprise, the forecasting director, a mathematical whiz, responded with “it is a people issue!”

A couple of months before Christmas the forecasting director had run an analysis of the connectivity in the forecasting community. It was brutally evident to him, why the forecasting of manufacturing was terrible.

The frontlines were disconnected from the regions. The regions were disconnected from each other. Knowledge and intelligence from the market was neither shared within and across regions, nor shared with the Forecasting Center of Excellence.

Everybody just minded their own business.

The Forecasting Center of Excellence was on the periphery of it all – while it was supposed to be at the center.

It consisted of about 15 highly educated individuals – some of the sharpest minds in the headquarters. The 15 individuals did not hide that they felt superior in expertise and intelligence. They saw themselves as the A-team.

Their arrogance was detrimental to the community.

Nobody wanted to ask them for their help and guidance in how to improve the forecasts or even to share any market intelligence with them at the risk of being mocked. They would rather stay quiet.

The Baseline of the Community Collaboration Was Astonishing

The CEO was astonished when the forecasting director showed him the illustration generated from his analysis of the community. It backed the words of the forecasting director.

NB! The picture shows regions by color. Dark grey is Europe. White is Asia. Light grey is the Americas. Black is the Center of Excellence.

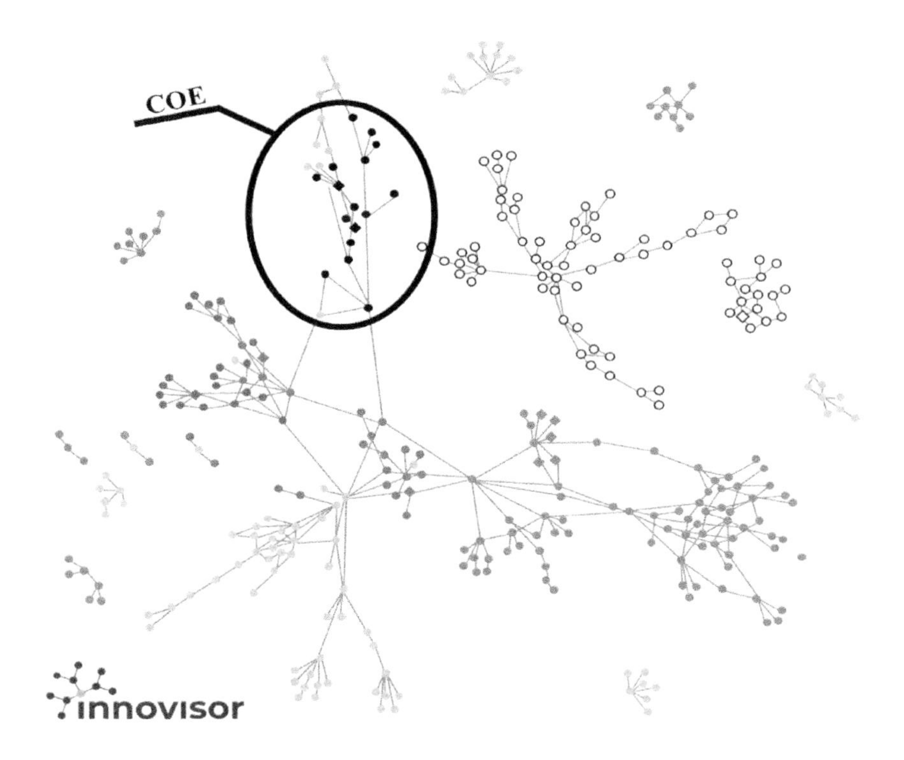

Network visual 10: The baseline of the community showed the Center of Excellence (COE) was not integrated.

"So, what is your plan?" – It was evident to the CEO that an IT system would not solve the problem. Not even if it was from SAP.

The Plan Was Simple, Focused, Cost-Effective, and Immediately Approved

The plan was simple, focused, cost-effective, and immediately approved.

- Use the baseline analysis to develop a target picture.

- Mobilize and engage the most influential employees in the regions around the change journey.
- Connect the regions at regional level by working with the right people.
- Connect the right people on the right areas of expertise.
- Transform the Center of Excellence into a humble, sympathetic & supportive group that the regions want to reach out to.
- Build mechanisms & principles for learning and knowledge sharing.

The Following Year Forecasting of the Christmas Sales Hit the Bullseye!

The forecasting director took charge of the change. He knew he needed to get his hands muddy if they were to succeed. But as he showed the baseline analysis to the community, and it was clear he had strong sponsorship from the CEO, things started to move.

18 months down the line he reran the analysis of the community to confirm his gut feeling that they were ready for the Christmas sales. He was happy to be able to report back to the CEO that the people issue was fixed.

The forecasting of the Christmas sales confirmed this.

It hit the bullseye!

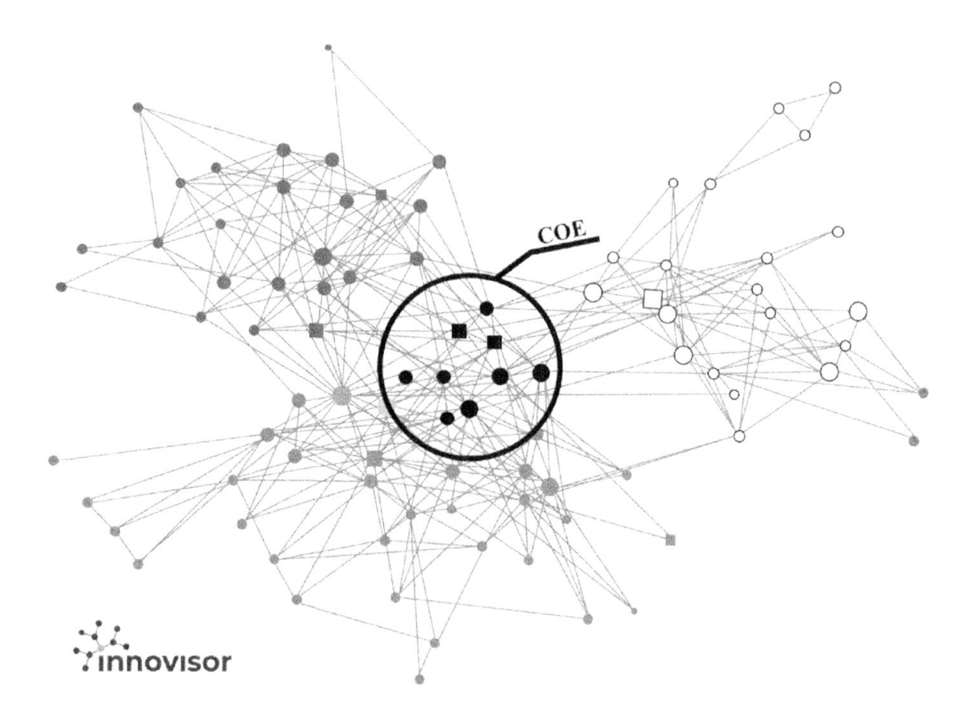

Network visual 11: The Center of Excellence (COE) regained its position in the collaboration network after two years.

Only two years later ManufacturingCo overtook the position as the leading company within its industry, and the CEO got recognized as the best CEO in the world.

This is one of the many successful case stories that I am most proud of in the history of Innovisor.

It proves beyond doubt why connecting people matters to success.

P.S. What happened to the forecasting director you might ask? He got hired by the main competitor and is redoing the same change exercise here. The results are evident. The stock market price of the competitor has improved 300% in only three years.

References

Literature

- BBC (2019) Dunbar's number: Why We Can Only Maintain 150 Relationships, available on: https://www.bbc.com/future/article/20191001-dunbars-number-why-we-can-only-maintain-150-relationships
- Blue, A. (2022) *Data Is Worthless Without Context*, in Forbes, 3 January 2022, available on: https://www.forbes.com/sites/forbestechcouncil/2022/01/03/data-is-worthless-without-context/
- Christakis, N.A., & Fowler, J.H. (2011) Connected: The Surprising Power of Our Social Networks and How They Shape Our Lives – How Your Friends' Friends' Friends Affect Everything You Feel, Think, and Do, Little Brown Spark, ISBN: 978-0316036139
- Colquitt, A. (2017) *Next Generation Performance Management: The Triumph of Science Over Myth and Superstition*, Information Age Publishing, ISBN: 978-1681239323
- Corporate Executive Board (2015) Are Lone Wolf Sales Reps Right for Your Organization, available on: https://www.cebglobal.com/blogs/are-lone-wolf-sales-reps-right-for-your-organization-2/

- Gardner, H. (2015) Why It Pays to Collaborate With Your Colleagues, in: The American Lawyer, available on: https://www.law.com/americanlawyer/almID/1202718495533/
- Grant, A. (2013) *Give and Take: Why Helping Other Drives Our Success*, Penguin Books, ISBN: 978-0315782143
- Grant, A. (2014) The Top Ten Signs You Might Be a Taker, available on: https://www.linkedin.com/pulse/20140320115939-69244073-the-top-ten-signs-you-might-be-a-taker/
- Hansgaard, J. (2015) Where is The Black Hole in Your Organization, available on: https://www.linkedin.com/pulse/where-black-hole-your-organization-jeppe-vilstrup-hansgaard/

- Hansgaard, J. (2018) Stop Breaking Down the Silos. Save Them!, available on: https://www.linkedin.com/pulse/stop-breaking-down-silos-save-them-jeppe-vilstrup-hansgaard/
- Hansgaard, J. (2019) The Danger Zones Where Your Scale-Up Fails, available on: https://www.linkedin.com/pulse/danger-zones-where-your-scale-up-fails-jeppe-vilstrup-hansgaard/
- Hansgaard, J. (2020) The Scale-Up That Almost Failed, available on: https://www.innovisor.com/2020/10/06/the-scale-up-that-almost-failed/

- Hansgaard, J. (2021) The Unharvested Potential of Organizational Bridges, available on: https://www.linkedin.com/pulse/unharvested-potential-organizational-bridges-jeppe-vilstrup-hansgaard/
- Hansgaard, J. (2022) Hybrid Work is Real – How we do it in Innovisor, available on: https://www.linkedin.com/pulse/hybrid-work-real-how-we-do-innovisor-jeppe-vilstrup-hansgaard/
- Hansgaard, J. (2023) Being International About 'WHO' is Key to Human-to-Human Connectivity, available on: https://www.linkedin.com/pulse/being-intentional-who-key-human-to-human-connectivity-hansgaard/
- Hansgaard, J. (2023) Massive Potential in Expertise Networks and Shadow Organizations, available on: https://www.linkedin.com/pulse/massive-potential-expertise-networks-shadow-jeppe-vilstrup-hansgaard/
- Hansgaard, J. (2023) Restructuring Does Not Remove Silos! People Do!, available on: https://www.linkedin.com/pulse/restructuring-does-remove-silos-people-do-jeppe-vilstrup-hansgaard/
- Hansgaard, J. (2023) Strong Hierarchies + Network Centricity = Amazing Results?, available on: https://www.linkedin.com/pulse/strong-hierarchies-network-centricity-amazing-results-hansgaard/

- Hansen, M.T. (2009) *Collaboration: How Leaders Avoid the Traps, Build Common Ground, and Reap Big Results*, Harvard Business Review Press, ISBN: 978-1422115152
- Hebert, P. (n.d.) Dunbar's Number and The Jetson Fallacy, available on: https://www.enterpriseengagement.org/articles/content/8468125/dunbars-number-and-the-jetson-fallacy/
- Innovisor (2018) From Misaligned Management to Realizing Full Potential, available on: https://www.innovisor.com/2018/04/18/from-misaligned-management-to-realizing-full-potential/
- Innovisor (2018) From Untapped Potentials to Effective Leadership Summit, available on: https://www.innovisor.com/2018/10/24/from-untapped-potentials-to-effective-leadership-summit/
- Innovisor (2019) Decision Making At the Core To Scale up As Organization, available on: https://www.innovisor.com/2019/11/27/from-being-a-start-up-to-a-scale-up/
- Innovisor (2023) How LifeScienceCo Improved Its Connectivity, available on: https://www.innovisor.com/2023/01/26/how-

lifescienceco-improved-its-connectivity-while-the-world-fell-apart/

- Innovisor (2023) The Right Thing to Do in a Hybrid Work Environment, available on: https://www.innovisor.com/2023/07/19/the-right-thing-to-do-in-a-hybrid-work-environment/
- Isaac, M. & McBurnie, A. (2015) *Close the Interaction Gap: Discover, Harness, and Accelerate the Collaborative Potential of your Leaders, Teams, and Organization*, Bridge Publishing, ISBN: 978-0986295607
- McChrystal, S. (2015) *Team of Teams: New Rules of Engagement for a Complex World*, Portfolio, ISBN: 978-1591847489
- Mikhail, A. (2023) Loneliness Is a Health Crisis Comparable to Smoking Up To 15 Cigarettes a Day. Here's How To Combat It, in: Fortune, available on: https://fortune.com/well/2023/06/15/loneliness-comparable-to-smoking-up-to-15-cigarettes-a-day/
- Mineo, L. (2017) Good Genes Are Nice, But Joy Is Better, in: The Harvard Gazette, available on: https://news.harvard.edu/gazette/story/2017/04/over-nearly-80-

years-harvard-study-has-been-showing-how-to-live-a-healthy-and-happy-life/

- Sandberg, S. (2013) *Lean In: Women, Work, and the Will to Lead*, Knopf, IBN: 978-0385349949
- Sull, D. & Sull, C. (2018) With Goals, FAST Beats SMART, in: MIT Sloan Review, available on: https://sloanreview.mit.edu/article/with-goals-fast-beats-smart/
- University of Kansas (2023) Just One Quality Conversation With a Friend Boosts Daily Well-Being, in ScienceDaily, available on: https://www.sciencedaily.com/releases/2023/02/230202135217.htm
- Vedres, B. & Vasarhelyi (2022) Inclusion Unlocks the Creative Potential of Gender Diversity in Teams, in: *Computer Science*, available on: https://arxiv.org/abs/2204.08505
- Wall Street Journal (2012) At Work, in: *Wall Street Journal*, available on: https://www.wsj.com/articles/SB10001424052702303506404577448652549105934

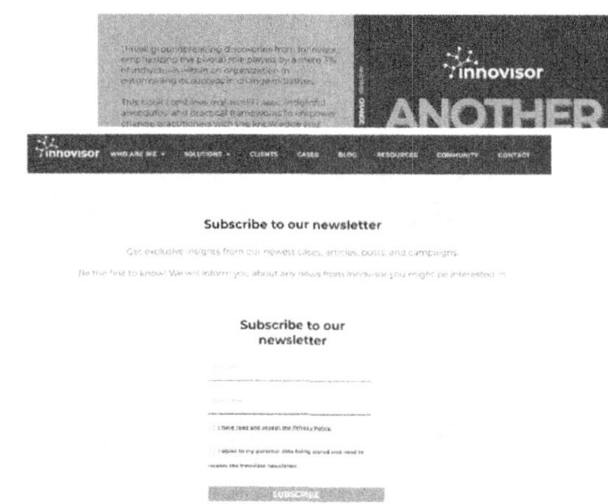

Subscribe to our newsletter to get latest updates on how to connect your people for better performance and wellbeing

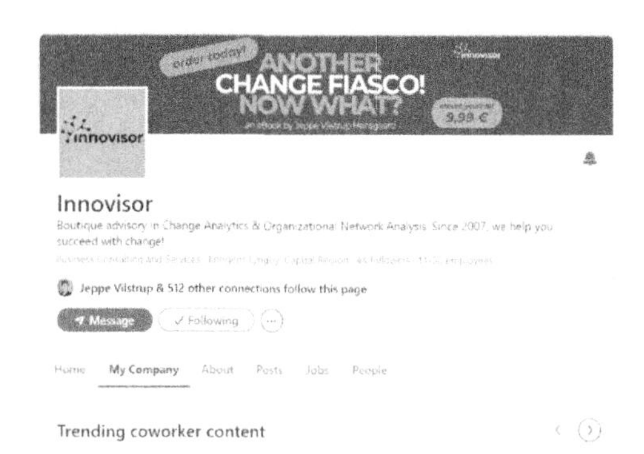

Follow us on our social media platforms such as LinkedIn and get notified on latest content

Printed in Great Britain
by Amazon